I0477607

Blockchain Technology:

Understanding the Technology behind Cryptocurrency, Blockchain's Limitless Potential and its Effects on Money and the World

David Vela

Table of Contents

Chapter 1 Introduction

Although most people automatically believe blockchain and bitcoin are the same thing, the reality is that bitcoin is only a manifestation of blockchain. Blockchain is essentially the platform that enables bitcoin, as well as other cryptocurrencies, to exist. Without it, these currencies would not have any basis and therefore they would not be usable.

Blockchain is essentially a decentralized database system that can store transaction data distributed across many different nodes. Because of the fact that it is decentralized, you do not actually have to physically travel to a location in order to complete a transaction. Instead, you can engage in the transaction virtually anywhere.

To break it down, imagine that you want to deposit money into your bank account. As a result, you visit your local branch and deposit the money. At that time, a transaction takes place and is recorded by the bank after they verify the authenticity of the payment. Your account is then updated to reflect the new deposit, and the money becomes available to you electronically.

Based on the current methods of transactions, the bank is inevitably always going to be involved. Even when you are processing a debit transaction at a retail location, the bank is involved in the process. Aside from the frustrations associated with having to have a third party present with everything, banks also carry other problems. Despite the amount of work that goes into keeping them secure and preventing manipulation, it cannot be completely manipulated. Additionally, that work itself is a drawback as it is costly to audit the banks and ensure that no manipulation is taking place. The current procedures are slow, can hold a variety of different errors, and are not completely safe from system tampering. Ultimately, they are becoming outdated.

The more society grows, the more important our currencies become. They are the basis for everything we do in life, whether we like to admit it or not. Even individuals who choose to live "off the grid" and attempt to avoid modern society are forced to use currency in order to acquire the things they need for their off-grid residencies. There is no denying the importance of currency. With currency comes transactions, and understandably you are going to want to have effective programs and systems in place to secure your transactions and ensure that there is no manipulation or tampering taking place with your money.

Blockchain is a program that has revolutionized the way transactions take place. It removes the requirement for third-party facilitators in transactions. Also, unlike banks where names and other potentially sensitive information is shared, blockchain maintains a level of anonymity to ensure that both parties involved in the transaction are further secured from any type of manipulation or tampering. Based off of the systems in place with blockchain, the transaction is authenticated, validated, and then approved and takes place. There are a series of cryptographic data signals that are involved in completing the transaction which makes it permanently approved and, in essence, completed. Then, the data is "hashed" onto the ledger of said node to form a chain of transaction records which cannot be hidden or erased.

The series of having the transactions stored on a chain where they cannot be erased adds an entire layer of security on its own. Due to the inability to erase or hide the chain, anyone who attempts to engage in fraudulent or illegal activities will be stopped immediately and the transaction will not take place. Ultimately, it is a completely secure foundation for transactions to take place.

How Transactions Are Verified

Blockchain has an ability to provide a high level of transparency behind transactions. Whenever transactions are verified by a node, every other node in the blockchain system is notified and therefore no transaction can be kept a secret. Every single node will have its system updated with the recent transaction, and it will not be possible to erase or hide the transaction. It will forever be linked to said person's name or code. Because all nodes are in agreeance with each other based on their histories, it is impossible to build a lie around a transaction, since they are clearly maintained and visible.

This is important because it is basically impossible to corrupt blockchain or commit fraud on the blockchain system. You cannot redirect payments to alternative accounts for money laundering, double-spend your money, or in any way increase the amount of money that is transferred to you or any other individual in any fraudulent way. Committing fraudulent activity on blockchain is virtually impossible to accomplish, and it is believed that it cannot be done. Aside from all of the technical complexities that would arise when you attempt to hack a node, you would not be able to change the transaction based on the decentralized program that blockchain is built on. There are several nodes that the transactions are inputted into, and you cannot change all of them through a single node. If you were able to hack a node and change a transaction on the node, the other nodes on the system would recognize the disagreement and the transaction would be halted as a result.

The entire system is also public, so anyone can see what has been done based on the transaction chains.

The Importance of Transparency in Transactions

Because of how blockchain functions, there is major transparency among all of the transactions that take place. All of these transactions can be located on a database that is viewable by the public, therefore all attempts at money laundering and committing fraudulent activities will be greatly reduced by the system. Any type of corruption around currency would be easily exposed and therefore it would be more difficult for large corporations and government to commit the fraud or corruption without being caught by the public. It ultimately democratizes the knowledge around transactions, which can have the ability to lead to more efficient markets.

At first, it may seem confusing to understand blockchain. It is a rather complex program that has taken computer scientists, mathematicians and cryptographers about a decade to compile. Rather than needing to understand the complexities of blockchain, the most important thing for you to understand is the way it works, how you can profit from it, and why blockchain is a revolution in and of itself. Understanding how powerful blockchain is and the number of changes it can make to modern society is important because it can assist you in understanding exactly why blockchain is important.

Chapter 2 History of the Blockchain

Although Satoshi Nakamoto, the creator of Bitcoin, takes home the trophy for creating the first widely accepted application using the blockchain technology, blockchain has a long history that came before him (he still takes home the trophy for creating the first usable form of blockchain. In fact, most of the applications using this technology today use what he was able to achieve as a benchmark).

In 1991, Stuart Haber and W. Scott Stornetta wrote a paper describing a cryptographically secure chain of block. In the following year, as a way to improve the efficiency of the ability to collect several of the documents into a block, the two introduced Merkle trees.

In 2008, Satoshi Nakamoto conceptualized the first distributed form of the blockchain. In the following year, he implemented it to create the currency Bitcoin. In Bitcoin, the blockchain served the purpose of being the management mechanism for the publicly distributed ledger for all financial transactions between peers. In this regard, the system used the peer-to-peer modeling and a distributed timestamp to make sure that the management of the Bitcoin database remained autonomous. The use of blockchain in the creation of Bitcoin proved the key to solving the problem of double spending, something very common with digital currencies in those days, without the need for secure administration.

In his initial paper published on 2008, Satoshi (the identity of Satoshi is still unknown. Some think he is a man living in Japan while others consider Satoshi a pseudonym for a group), used the terms block and chain on separate occasions and as separate terms. When others started using what he had achieved, they used the term block chain and in 2016, the term became one: blockchain.

In 2014, just six years after the conceptualization of Bitcoin, the first app running on the blockchain technology (Bitcoin and blockchain are not mutually exclusive and as you now know, Bitcoin is not the only use of the blockchain technology), the size of the Bitcoin blockchain stood at over 20 gigabytes. As use of the currency increased, the size of the file increased to over 30 gigabytes by January of the following year (2015), a size that had grown to over 100 gigabytes by 2017.

2014 brought with it a new term: blockchain 2.0, a term used to refer to applications (other than Bitcoin) using the blockchain technology called Ethereum. An Op-ed piece published on The Economist described the implementation of these new generation apps as follows: "blockchain 2.0 is a sort of programming language that allows users to write sophisticated smart contracts. These smart contracts allow for the creation of invoices that pay themselves upon the arrival of a shipment or share certificates that automatically send their owners dividends if profits reach a certain level."

While this definition is very true, application of blockchain 2.0 applications goes beyond transaction. They allow for the exchange of value on a peer-to-peer basis without the explicit need of powerful intermediaries such as banks acting as arbiters or keeping records of transactions or information. These applications allow those who would otherwise not have access to global currencies such as the dollar or pound to play an equal part in global trade and economy. Through smart contracts and cryptography, these platforms also foster privacy protection (which is why in its early days, criminals on the Silk Road website used Bitcoin as their preferred means of trade).

Applications that use blockchain 2.0 make the storage of a person's individual ID and persona easier and secure; because of this, they are helping shape future monies, distribution of wealth, and ease wealth inequality.

A Chronological Development of Blockchain Related Technologies

We cannot fail to mention that in the 10 years the blockchain innovation has been in existence, it has gone through some changes and seen the introduction of various new technologies that have made it what it is today. Here is a chronological view of these changes:

1.   The first major innovation of the technology occurred when Satoshi introduced Bitcoin, the first successful application to use the blockchain technology. Introduced in a world in dire need of a decentralized currency, wide adoption of Bitcoins has seen their market cap rise to over $20 billion. Today, thousands of people across the world are using this blockchain-based currency to make payments and online purchases.

2.   After the development of Bitcoin came the realization that the underlying technology could apply to many other areas and that the technology itself was not synonymous with Bitcoins. Many world-leading financial institutions are currently researching how they can integrate the technology into their financial offerings and in-house applications. According to research by Fortune.com, about 15% of all major banks are looking into how they can integrate the technology into their processes.

3.   The third major innovation in blockchain development was the introduction of smart contracts. Simply put, a smart contract is a computer-based protocol whose aim is to

facilitate, enforce, and verify contractual negotiations. Of all smart contracts introduced, the Ethereum blockchain platform is the most prominent one; we shall discuss its development and application later. Ethereum built multiple, 2nd gen programs into the blockchain platform to allow for the transfer of loans, bonds, and other financial instruments. The development of Ethereum came out of necessity.

4.   The 4th innovation, which is what many blockchain 2.0 applications in existence today use, is proof of stake. Applications such as Bitcoin (the current version of it), use something called proof of work. In the blockchain world, proof of work is data that is easy to verify based on certain requirements but that is difficult or costly to produce. Proof of work produced the aspect of mining where a computer or group of networked computers with the most computing power would make the decisions in that since they had the most power, they could provide secure proof of work faster for all blockchain transactions such as cryptocurrencies transfers or payments. For their services, these computers earn cryptocurrencies; this explains why cryptocurrency mining has become popular.

These four are the main developmental stages of blockchain. Experts also agree that in the days to come, another revolutionary innovation that is going to change the blockchain technology is blockchain scaling. Here is how this shall pan out.

We have already established that a blockchain is a decentralized, peer-to-peer managed ledger upon which the transactions recorded by the computers on the network reside. As we have also seen, processing these transactions uses the computing power of every computer in the network, something that has proven slow and rather expensive to manage (which is why cryptocurrency mining is not as lucrative as it once used to be).

Because of the above, blockchain scaling, a new form of blockchain innovation, is on the horizon. This innovation intends to accelerate the rate at which the computers on the network record the data into blocks, all this without sacrificing the security or integrity of the block. To do this, blockchain scaling intends to interrogate the network to determine the number of computers needed to validate individual transactions and using this base number, divide the work equally among all the computers in the network. As you can imagine, this will lead to increased efficiency. This technology, if it comes to fruition, which is likely to be very soon, will rival technologies such as SWIFT and VISA, and play an integral role in powering the internet of things.

The above is a representation of how blockchain has changed in the last 10 years thanks to the work of an elite group of mathematicians, cryptographers, and computer scientists working to improve this disruptive innovation. As the innovation continues to improve, it is changing many things about how we live our everyday life. For instance, many experts in the field opine that as these breakthroughs come through, the future may see us using blockchain technologies to pay for services such as charging stations and landing pads for self-driving cars and drones.

Now that we are talking about how the blockchain technology is changing the future of money, we cannot fail to discuss Ethereum, the other blockchain innovation that is changing our perception of the blockchain as a predominantly currency-development technology. Before we do that, however, let us discuss the benefits of the blockchain technology.

Chapter 3 Basic Terms Used in Blockchain

Before we plunge straight into the other essential information about the blockchain, let me familiarize you with some of the commonly used basic terms in blockchain. These terms may be defined again in some chapters, but I decided to compile them in one chapter, as a quick reference.

Blockchain

A public or private ledger distributed to people in the blockchain's network.

Peer-to-Peer (P2P) networking

A decentralized network, where peer-to-peer (direct user to user) transactions occur, without the mediation of a third party.

Public Key

This is a cryptograph or code utilized by a blockchain user to verify that the other user is the actual person he is dealing with. It's used to verify the user's private key.

Private Key

This is a cryptograph or code that can verify that the user is definitely who he claims he is. You can use your private key to access your wallet where your cryptocurrency is stored. If you lose this key, you cannot enter your black box or wallet, thus, you will lose private data and your digital money as well. Subsequently, you can create another black box, but you can never recover your money in the original box, if you don't have your own private key.

Node

You and your computer are nodes because you are the one running, reading, writing and downloading blocks through your own computer.

Proof-of-work (PoW)

Proof-of-work is accomplished when a miner solves a math problem. When this is done, the new block is added to the chain. Miners are usually paid in digital currency as incentives in solving the problem. When the majority of the nodes in the network approves of the solution, all the nodes are updated with the new block. PoW also grants a 'right' to participate in the blockchain network.

Proof-of-stake (PoS)

This is intended to be an alternative for proof-of-work. It's a consensus algorithm, that stems from the holdings of the cryptocurrency. PoS eliminates the 51% attack. The 51% attack involves the acquisition of 51% computing power by a hacker, and then using this to control the network. This is almost impossible, however, because the bitcoins in circulation are not equal to 51% of Bitcoin. Between PoW and PoS, PoS is tougher to compromise.

Transaction

A transaction deals with assets, usually financial, that blockchain users engage in. But asset may not concern only money but anything of value to the users (data, information, properties (tangible and intangible), and similar items.

Contract

This is an agreement that details the condition of the transaction between users. It specifies the business terms or what is expected from both parties. If the expectations are not fulfilled, the process of what would happen must be itemized and explicitly stated, so that it can be executed automatically.

Hash

A hash is used to connect the new block to the previous block to make it tamper-proof. All blocks are 'hashed' together to ensure the validity, legitimacy and trueness of the block. In short, it acts as a unique digital fingerprint. Hash codes are used to secure transactions through cryptography.

Cryptocurrency

This is the currency (digital money) used in blockchain transactions, where encryption of algorithms confirms the transactions.

Digital currency

This is the currency used in online transactions. It may not be necessarily a cryptocurrency.

Assets

Assets can be tangible (house, car, store) and intangible (music, stories, bonds, patents), and are usually used in blockchain transactions. These are items that can produce value that can be owned by users.

Ledger

This is where transactions are recorded. In blockchain, the shared ledger is the same. It's also where blockchain transactions are recorded. Only, it's now shared and distributed to all members of the network.

Block

This is considered a 'page' where permanent files are recorded. They are usually in chronological order, according to time. These connecting blocks make up the blockchain.

Consensus

Consensus is the general agreement of the users about the validity of a block, or a solution to an issue. This ensures that the blockchain is protected because of the provision of exact copies to all users in the blockchain network. This is done through the shared ledgers. Any tampering of the blocks can be confirmed if the block doesn't appear simultaneously in all the distributed ledgers. Consensus is said to have been reached, if all the blocks in all shared and distributed ledgers are identical.

Decentralization

This is the process of eliminating intermediaries and spreading the power or responsibility among all users of a blockchain network. This denotes that no one owns the chain, and not any one person can control it.

Internet of Things (IoT)

This encompasses the continuously growing interconnection of a global network of physical and virtual devices or apps and the values/assets or data they communicate to each other on the Internet.

These are some terms that you may come across with when you are reading about blockchain. This is not complete because there are numerous terms involving blockchain, but these are the most common.

Chapter 4 Components of the Basic Design of Blockchain

All platforms using the blockchain technology is recommended to have the major components of its basic design. This is due to the fact that the blockchain involves value transfer and the exchange of valuable data or information.

For blockchain to be a success, these components must be present in its basic design. These include the following:

Security

Blockchain can never operate without adequate security. Its design is made in such a way that the design becomes a security feature in itself.

Nonetheless, in this era of Internet explosion and state-of-the-art technology, there will always be issues about security. Premier banks worry about their security. Well-known websites worry about their security. In other words, it's an unending and widespread problem.

Therefore, blockchain is no exception. Most private blockchain platforms/systems are adding extra features to the existing blockchain security to ensure that their systems are secure.

Privacy

The privacy of users is protected through the use of public and private keys. You can refer to the previous chapters on how these keys (secret codes) are generated and used, and how privacy is protected with the use of the black box. The black box is where all the user's private information and data are stored. Only the user with his blockchain ID can access his blackbox. An example of a blockchain ID is 9b3cae0-67b1-56gc-a3c7-g328a2bcfcf7. This is entered together with the password, before a user can access his blockchain account.

Network Integrity

The integrity of your network is essential for a blockchain system to succeed. The trust protocol is what develops a network that you can trust. Each node must be honest, and expects other nodes to be honest as well. The strength of a blockchain lies in its weakest link.

Decentralization

Decentralization is one of the vital advantages of blockchain. This process allows network users to have control over their assets, and to trade, sell, or do whatever they wish - without the interference of mediators. In this regard, all the users in the blockchain network are on equal footing.

Financial Inclusion

This deals with users who have no bank accounts for various reasons. They have to be included in the blockchain network. There are billions of people using the Internet who still don't have basic bank accounts because they lack documents, such as birth certificates, that could support their identity. It could also be because they don't have the amount of money needed for an initial deposit. Whatever the reason, you have to make sure that 'inclusion' is one of the features of the blockchain.

Using blockchain so that these people can be included in the network will be advantageous to both the concerned countries and the 'unbanked' people.

In the absence of a computer, people can use mobile phones to connect to the blockchain. Mobile banking is largely recognized by almost all countries, and the inclusion of a blockchain in the banks' systems would allow these 'unbanked' people to be able to open accounts without presenting documents.

The inclusion need not be financial only. It could also be in other aspects of society, where people need to transact business - but could not, because they lack proper documentation, or pertinent papers (example: refugees).

Blockchain can allow users to create their digital identity without their proper documents.

With these in mind, it's safe to conclude that the blockchain system can create a new world, where everyone can be included and be fairly treated. Inequality will be eschewed because everyone has equal opportunities in the network. This system will encourage an open, fair and inclusive economy, thus, has the propensity of wealth redistribution.

Rights preserved

Each user's right must be preserved by the blockchain. Each member of the blockchain is an important block in the chain. If one is broken, all the other blocks will be disconnected, affecting the entire blockchain. Therefore, the rights of each member must be preserved and respected.

Value as incentive

In some blockchain platforms, incentives are given to miners. These incentives come in the value of cryptocurrencies or digital money. Most blockchain sites have similar rules with regards to granting incentives using their own digital coins.

Since the open source code of the blockchain technology has become available to the public for free, numerous sites/platforms have sprouted and used the code. Some of them have modified or developed the blockchain to suit their purposes. The basic components, though, must be integrated.

Chapter 5 Harnessing Global Integrity

For blockchain to work properly, integrity should exist between users. Bear in mind that there are no third parties to mediate. Hence, each user must be responsible and honest with his transactions. This can be possible with the establishment of global integrity. This means that every user around the world is watching all the transactions that are done. So, it would be difficult to intentionally commit mistakes with the purpose of deceiving another user.

For all digital transactions, each blockchain user is expected to adhere to the principles of integrity.

What is integrity?

Integrity is the ability or quality to be true, honest and accurate about one's deeds. It indicates the ethical and moral responsibility of a person to himself and to other people.

How can integrity be demonstrated in blockchain transactions?

The integrity of the user can be demonstrated through his honesty, transparency, accountability and concern for other users in his dealings. Honesty is being upfront with what the other user can benefit or lose from the transaction.

On the other hand, transparency is the trait of being able to allow the other users to see the transactions you are doing in your own node. This doesn't mean that all users can see your personal and private information, remember, these are encrypted. What other users can see, is the summary of your transaction.

Accountability is to be held responsible for contracts agreed on, or being able to take responsibility for the consequences of one's actions. Concern about the other users can focus on the law of 'karma'. 'What goes around comes around' is an apt cliché to describe this behavior. 'Karma' is a law of nature. You will surely receive what you have 'given' to other people.

The rule of 'karma' can be demonstrated in this simple occurrence. Throw a stone into a stagnant lake and observe how the ripples of waves go outwards, and then back inwards again. In this regard, each user must not attempt to rip off other users, if he doesn't want to be ripped off in return.

When all blockchain users observe these traits, then cryptocurrency transactions will become a resounding success.

How does transparency occur in blockchains?

When I talk about transparency, I'm talking about transparency in your digital transactions. It's understandable that extremely private information or data are not revealed to other users. Only, what you want to be disclosed will be shown. How can this be done? You can create your digital business persona, or another persona that will deal with other aspects of your blockchain transactions. All your personal information is placed in a special box, which you can monetize any way you want. For example, you can monetize your data about your favorite movies by participating in an online survey.

To secure your identity, a specific 'key' is assigned to you, and only you can open your box with that key. So, you control the revelation of your information. With that unique 'key', blockchain helps you protect your identity.

While protecting your identity, you are expected to participate actively as a node. You and your computer constitute a node. Say for example on Bitcoin, as a node in a public blockchain, you can do the following:

- Download and store the blockchain free core software

- Listen, validate and pass on transactions

- Listen, validate and pass on blocks

- Mine and create blocks

Your transactions are secured using the public key and your own private keys. Bear in mind that the security of your private key is your responsibility alone. You should not divulge it to anyone. Your previous transactions will serve as another method to confirm your identity.

Also, you can prevent hackers from stealing your blockchain account by: adding a phone number and email address, so that when there are changes, you can be notified promptly. Use the two-factor authorization/authentication too, where you have to add an extra password.

As more global users transact their businesses on blockchain, global integrity can be gradually achieved.

Chapter 6 The Issue of Trust within Blockchain

The issue of trust in blockchain is critical to its success. Since the onset of the Internet, online transactions have increasingly spiraled. This is done through the assistance of third parties, such as PayPal and similar companies. The trust established with these companies was teetering though, because of the danger of private and personal information being compromised or leaked by hackers.

This is not only true in financial companies but also on social media sites. Reportedly, Facebook alone has more than 300 petabytes of private information from its users. For now, Facebook (FB) has successfully protected the private data of its users.

However, if you notice the ads being displayed when you sign in into your account, you will know that FB knows your interests and preferences. It's monetizing your private information legally, and it's earning big money from these data. This is why it's possible for FB to provide incredible apps in its site and provide them to you – for free.

In blockchain, the problem of your private information being disclosed won't likely occur anymore. This is because the transactions are conducted only between the persons doing the transactions - without the assistance of third parties. You can now monetize your own information too, if you want. It's up to you.

But how does blockchain ensure security within its technology? How can it ascertain that the user's identity and private information is secure and safe? How can you trust blockchain and how can other blockchain users trust you?

1.   First, to gain trust, you must be trustworthy.

The transactions you conduct, your location, and the contacts you deal with are evidences of your identity. You may not be aware of it but you leave your 'footprints' around the Internet with your comments, your posts, your membership in sites, your searches, the videos you watch, the games you play, your time stamps, and similar activities. These are all 'recorded' by the World Wide Web and taken advantage of by big companies to earn money. Your digital identity comes from your online activities.

In the blockchain technology, users, as nodes, are expected to be trustworthy. If you're not trustworthy, other users can see your wrongdoing. It's like you're playing on the world stage where your every movement is recorded, and every one can see what you're up to. So, you cannot change entries, or enter into spurious transactions without anyone noticing the activity on the real-time worldwide ledger.

As you do more transactions with other users and establish more relationships, your identity grows together with your trustworthiness. It is believed that the more you pour work into the system, the less likely you'll cheat. Hence, you as a node in the blockchain, becomes a legitimate measure of other nodes that you associate with.

2.   In blockchain, YOU control your own data using a private key.

You can use as many pseudonyms as you want. Every time you perform a transaction, you are asked to enter your personal private 'key', known only to you. In essence, there are two keys that you have to use. The first is the public key, which can correspond to your user ID, when you sign in to regular sites, and the private key, which can correspond to your password. However, it's not as simple as it appears. These public and private keys are not as easy as using your user ID and password. Examples of the public keys are SHA256 (reportedly used by US government) and RIPEMD160.

The keys are cryptographic (cipher text) in nature that is unreadable to viewers. Only you, as the user, or owner of the data can decrypt the cipher text to a readable form using your private key. You should keep your private key a secret, but you can reveal your public key.

You can call this the black box or your personal wallet, which contains all your pertinent and private information.

3. The use of the Trust Formula.

Some blockchain private users have created a Trust Formula that is used to compute for the trust score for every node in the blockchain. This formula is based on the blockchain's purpose. Generally, random nodes are selected to be used in the formula. The formula involves the good and bad actions the user (node) performs, and then turning this into a probability through the sigmoid function.

The sigmoid function or sigmoidal curve is a logistic (planning or implementation) mathematical function that usually takes an S- shape curve.

This may start to sound so technical, so, I'll simply say, that these sigmoid curves can illustrate progress of innovations, business cycles and to 'squash' (reduce into a small number) responses to keep the data within bounds and come up with a probability. This will then provide a clue into the trustworthiness of the node (user).

I would like to present the formula, but I know it would confuse some readers, so I'll skip it. Anyway, you won't be computing the formula yourself, the blockchain technology will do it for you - automatically.

To give you a visual picture of what a blockchain is, you can imagine an endless, interconnected chain that goes on and on. As they are interconnected with each other; you cannot remove or alter one chain without affecting all the other blocks. Since it's also public, anyone can see whatever alterations are being done. The bad node will have to alter everything from the start of the chain until the current block, which is nearly impossible. The link is growing faster and longer that the bad node won't be able to catch up.

4.   Tamper-proof distributed ledgers and identity

As explained earlier the blockchain acts as a public world ledger, and the data entered are immutable (unchangeable). Users cannot tamper with the data because they are interconnected to each other, up to the very first transaction. The ledgers are distributed too, to each user, so any changes would be updated real-time into all of the distributed ledges, hence, it could not be altered. It's like – each node in the block has the ability to look out for each other. Your identity is also tamper-proof (please refer to the previous discussions).

5.   Use of several codes and hashes

In addition, Blockchain codes are used in securing the users' privacy through the use of cryptography. There's a code used in generating a compound identity; another code is used in gaining permission for entry into the blockchain; the third code is for the access control protocol; and the fourth code for the loading and storing of data.

In the event that another person tries to change or utilize another user's private key, the hash will act as a trap to stop the process. The hashes should match to ensure that the message is not altered and that the key is correct. If the hash is altered, it indicates that the private key is wrong. Only your key can encrypt the hash of the message to confirm or sign that you own the message.

6.   Use of Smart Contracts

This is a computer programmable code contained in the blockchain, which can be executed when the user fulfills certain conditions. This is one way that the blockchain in bitcoin and other platforms protect and secure the data and identity of users or nodes. These contracts are replicated and shared in the ledger that is available to all users.

Reportedly, there were instances in the past, in which tests were done to introduce unrelated data to the blockchain using bots, or software turned into malware. This is one possibility that can introduce potential harm to the blockchain security system. This development will surely prompt blockchain users to develop more technology, on top of the blockchain technology, to ensure that the security of the information provided and the identity of the nodes (users) are safe.

In addition, in blockchain, trust is established using mass consensus or confirmation, plus, the utilization of clever codes that have to be decrypted.

Chapter 7 The Blockchain Revolution

The future of blockchain is the essence of the blockchain revolution. In just one decade, it has come incredibly far and has left so many changes in its path. Like the internet or the smartphone, blockchain is a system that is believed to be heading in a direction that will make massive changes to our entire way of life. You will likely find that blockchain will change everything from the way we sell art and products to the way we manage finances and purchase goods. There are many ways that blockchain technology can have a major impact on our future.

As we have discussed periodically throughout this book, blockchain has the ability to bring about a great amount of security with it. Because of this, there is a huge potential to greatly reduce the risks attached to the online space. Identity authentication will be offered through a public ledger that makes it easier for people to be caught when they are committing fraudulent activities. There are already requirements attached around numbering, maintaining and indexing records around transactions, and the information that is provided in the records need to be communicated from time to time, as well. This is especially true when you are working with different financial services to assist you with certain activities. Having a blockchain system storing all of this information would make it more easily accessible, as well as it would increase the security and efficiency around the storing of the information.

There are many other things that can be controlled, as well. For example, if blockchain technology was more widespread, pieces of physical property could be attached to the blockchain system and could perform incredible functions on its own. Fridges, for example, could be equipped with sensors that allow them to order and pay for food, as well as arrange software upgrades. In addition, it could track its own warranty, so if something was wrong it would be able to make a claim and then the appropriate servicing department would come out to assist you in fixing your fridge. This could be true for many things, beyond just fridges. Cars could be hybridized and parked on specific parking pads that would charge them, and they would automatically pay for their charges. Your car could track its own warranties and any things associated with it that may need to be repaired or fixed. There are several items that could benefit from being connected to a blockchain system with sensors and internet connection. This type of connection would enable many of your pieces of technology to be self-sufficient and would require minimal maintenance on your behalf to keep the system functioning properly.

On a business end, small businesses would have the ability to use the sophisticated blockchain technology to create their own trusted trading platforms which they could then trade among other small businesses. The corporate trading industry would no longer be restricted to only large corporations, but rather any business who wanted to get involved. This would open up a great opportunity to help bring transparency to the trading environment, especially the post-trade section. Based on the speed of blockchain technology, the timing associated with investment risks would be completely altered. Trading as we know it would be completely different from what it is now.

Another reason why the speed of blockchain would be incredible is that it would alter the speed at which the bank is able to pay suppliers. Payments could be made instantly, which could make the rate at which things are done much quicker. People would no longer have to wait for transactions to be approved and authenticated and then released because these fulfillments would be done instantly.

Blockchain would also have a major impact on crime. Based on the methodology behind blockchain, there are people who are claiming that they can use this system to track down criminals faster than ever. Additionally, this service would be cheaper than existing tracking services. There would be less waiting to catch criminals and fewer criminals on the streets being left to their own devices. Anyone who committed a crime would be much more likely to be identified, caught, and forced to serve their justice.

There are some complications that arise when it comes to integrating blockchain with banks. These risks are currently the reason why many banks have hesitated to get completely on board with the new system. Many banks, however, are investing in learning more about these technologies to see how they can alter the risk and turn it into a positive. If banks were to adopt blockchain technology, it is not surprising that cryptographically secured currencies would spread rapidly and become more widely used in the everyday world. They would become more prominent in the trading and investment environment, as well as more commonly used with transactions. Blockchain technology also has the ability to completely eliminate the need for centralized banks. Since the system is infinitely more secure and efficient, physical bank locations would cease to exist due to a floundering need for their presence. Still, the real risks associated with banks would remain present, even if the banks were to be transitioned over to the blockchain technologies.

Other amazing things associated with banks becoming involved in blockchain technologies is that the costs associated with securities trading, cross-border payments, and regulatory compliance could be greatly reduced. It would be much less costly for them to complete the transactions and therefore they could save as much as $20 billion by the year 2022. The number of applications that would be associated within' and outside of centralized banks would be greatly reduced, as well. Blockchain transactions would contain all relevant information for transfers to be successful, and therefore there would be no need for such a high volume of paperwork and contract signings to be associated with transactions.

Some people, however, do not see blockchain as being a positive. Some banks believe that this system could be dangerous as there simply isn't enough IT infrastructure available to support the system. If anything were ever to go wrong with it, there wouldn't be enough knowledgeable minds to fix it. Additionally, if the system was down for any amount of time, it would have the potential to be compromised and it would cause serious backlash on the markets. They believe that the blockchain system might just be the opportunity for another cartel to be opened and that it will be dominated by cryptocurrencies. These banks believe that blockchain would fail to be able to function effectively enough to operate everyday payments, which is a major part of banking for the majority of people.

Blockchain technology has the potential to completely change the face of financial infrastructure as we know it. Smart contracts, smart property, and other blockchain-based applications would completely change the way the systems functioned and there would be no need for existing methods to be used anymore. Ultimately, it could completely bypass the way our financial systems currently operate and change the face of the financial world entirely. Nothing would be untouched by the system, from trading and transactions to sales and everyday banking.

Many other industries would be greatly impacted by the blockchain systems, as well. While these industrial changes have not been as deeply explored as the financial industry's changes have been, they still exist. Ultimately, it will be up to those industries to really see how exactly blockchain systems can have an impact on their businesses. Still, it is inevitable that they will be directly affected by the system.

One way that blockchain is guaranteed to have an impact on various industries is through transaction processes. Virtually every industry has an underlying financial structure, and this structure will not be immune to the changes that blockchain will bring about. It is, however, believed that blockchain would have a highly positive impact on these industries. For example, these businesses would not have to rely on third parties to facilitate transactions within' their business. Instead, it would all be done through blockchain systems. This would completely change the face of business banking.

In addition to changing the financial structure of the business and the way transactions are facilitated, blockchain would have the ability to create entirely new business opportunities. Existing technologies and processes would be completely disrupted, but as a result, there would be entirely new opportunities available. People could use blockchain as a trading post, they could rent the excess cloud storage, and they could become trained as blockchain consultants to assist others in navigating the blockchain environment. There would be many other careers opened up too, as a result.

Blockchain would have the opportunity to completely shrink the world as we know it. The boundaries between countries and businesses would be completely eliminated. Transactions and trades across the board would be easier than ever to facilitate, and there would be much less difficulty when working with businesses from anywhere. Transactions would be instant and businesses could interact overseas just as effortlessly as they would if they were direct next-door neighbors.

Ultimately, the face of business would completely change. Models behind businesses would change, career opportunities would open up, and trading would become much easier. Businesses large and small would all have fair chances at the same opportunities, and there would be almost nothing keeping small businesses from having the same impact as large businesses currently do. Smaller businesses would be opened up to opportunities to have a major impact on the world and take their business from a local market to a global and universal market.

In addition to banks and business, blockchain would also have a massive impact on governments. If blockchain were to be completely integrated, traditional currencies as we know it could be eliminated entirely. Instead of having different currencies for different nations, we would have bitcoin and other cryptocurrencies that would dominate the market. There would be no need for country- or region-specific currencies. As well, blockchain would be an excellent way to distribute currencies to developing nations in order to assist in raising social welfare and ensuring that everyone across the globe was taken care of. We would be able to eliminate the boundaries and lines across countries and come together as one united global community.

Another powerful way that blockchain would have the ability to impact government is through elections. As we have already explored, blockchain could be used to eliminate the expenses and time investment in elections. Instead of having to fund expensive election facilities and hire and train the people to run them, everything could be done instantaneously online. This would increase the speed, improve voter turnout, and decrease the costs associated with elections.

The idea of self-driving cars, fridges that order and pay for food, and technology that can completely self-service itself was once a mere dream of a futuristic society. People dreamt up a vast number of incredible changes that society would endure if technology advanced to such a space, and in the meantime computer scientists, cryptographers and mathematicians were in the process of turning those dreams into a reality. Blockchain is the system that is bringing us forward into this futuristic society in the fastest way possible. Just a decade ago, blockchain was only a dream. It rapidly became a reality, however, and it continues to hurdle forward to be the new potential for our society. Time will only tell how far this blockchain revolution actually goes, but it is clear that it isn't about to stop anytime soon.

Chapter 8 Benefits of the Blockchain Technology

Other than being the backbone upon which cryptocurrencies such as Bitcoin rest, the blockchain technology has a vast number of uses whose benefits surpasses that of cryptocurrencies and their creation. Let us discuss some of these benefits before we discuss Ethereum in the next section.

The need for blockchain is not as evident as it would be because as many postulate, you can use a software or platform such as Google or databases to record transactions. While databases have no fault, blockchain has proven effectual and beneficial. Here are some of its key benefits:

Fully Distributed

This is one of the key benefits of the blockchain technology. As illustrated many times in this guide, participants in any blockchain application, perhaps Bitcoin mining or trading, will have access to a copy of the most current blockchain.

Mining of the currencies that use these technologies is also distributed. This means that at any point in time, no computer (no matter how powerful it is) can dominate the network. If that were the case, the most powerful computers would do all the mining and hog all the created currencies leaving none for the hobby miner. The distributed nature of the blockchain makes this impossible.

Use of Decentralized Verification

We have discussed how currencies and applications that use the blockchain technology are decentralized. This aspect of the innovation eliminates the need for a central authority such as a central bank; having to take transactions through a central database can be limiting in terms of the time it takes for the transaction to happen.

Enhanced Security

In a widely corrupt internet where some people use blackhat strategies to trick users into giving them their bank and credit card information, an anonymous way of paying for goods and services proves very helpful. Since many online buyers are seeking anonymity above all else, they are turning to blockchain powered currencies such as Bitcoins and Ether since these currencies use cryptographically secure, complex algorithms to record all transactions without compromising personal identity. To make and receive blockchain-powered currencies, all you need is an address. This reduces the risk of fraud.

Enhanced Trust among Parties

Blockchain offers top-level security features (using cryptographic code). This increases the level of trust between those transacting. Further, because there is zero exchange of value, and records of the transactions remain on the blockchain under all circumstances, the level of trust between those sending cryptocurrencies and those receiving it increases.

Low Entry Barrier

This is one of the key benefits of the blockchain innovation: it allows anyone to use the network—anyone who has an internet connected computer or smartphone can use blockchain and Bitcoins as long as he or she downloads the client software.

Real-time Transactional Capabilities

Waiting for three or more days for a transaction to reflect on your bank or account statement is a pain many users are keen to avoid whenever they can —today's consumers want immediate results after making any purchase: they want the transaction to reflect on their accounts almost immediately.

The blockchain technology makes it possible to make payments immediately or within 10 minutes, which when you consider the time it takes for credit cards to process transactions, is the best option currently available.

Enhanced Global Operations and Trade

Considering that we live in an interconnected world where someone in America can be in business with someone living at the farthest point in Africa, the need for speedy transactions has never been higher. Blockchain based currencies enhance this intercontinental trade by enhancing the speed of transactions and reducing the fees levied on sending monies from one person or business to the other.

Eliminates the Problem of Double Spending

This is something we discussed earlier as one of the key advantages of the blockchain technology. We have also mentioned that applications using the blockchain use cryptography to secure the system and prevent the duplication of transaction (especially monetary ones) to make sure that users of the system do not produce money out of thin air.

The system processes each transaction once before entering it into a block and linking the block to the chain. Once processed and recorded into the blockchain, the system cannot process that transaction again; this eliminates the redundancy so common with the records of most modern banking systems. Further, because the arrangement of the blocks uses a linear and chronological manner, tracking transactions becomes dummy-easy.

Low Transaction Costs

One of the main reasons why the uptake of cryptocurrencies such as Bitcoins and Litecoins has been on the rapid rise is the fact that most of these currencies have the lowest transfer rates imaginable. This plays in very well with consumers who are looking to save money on transactional fees as they shop.

The links below show how to calculate transactional fees for ether and Bitcoins.

https://ethereum.stackexchange.com/questions/19665/how-to-calculate-transaction-fee

https://en.bitcoin.it/wiki/Transaction_fees

https://bitcoinfees.21.co/

Those advocating for, and spearheading the use of, the blockchain technology are quick to point out that the applicability of the innovation goes beyond that of Bitcoin or financial transactions. For instance, many of those involved are quick to point out that the blockchain shall play an integral role in elections of the future (read more here).

Still, like every new technology, there are those who feel that the technology has its fair share of drawbacks, especially its ability to accommodate the rapid uptake and increased number of transactions. Since most applications that use this technology create an average of 61 new blocks every 10 minutes, each individual system creates an average of 144 blocks per day. To the cautious, this is something they consider problematic because it may influence the storage and speed of transaction, which may lead to update and synchronization issues.

Let us flesh out some of the drawbacks of the blockchain technology and discuss their possible solutions:

Chapter 9 Disadvantages of Using Blockchain Technology

While the blockchain has many uses and an immense number of benefits, it also has its drawbacks. In this subsection, we shall look at these disadvantages as well as how to overcome them:

Performance

The first issue many are quick to point out is the issue of performance. Some experts in the field of finance point out that compared to the speed of centralized databases especially in relation to transaction records, the blockchain is slower because on top of recording a transaction as a normal database does, it also has to do three other things:

1. Verify signature: Every blockchain transaction must have a digital signature that uses a public-private cryptographic scheme (a good example is the ECDSA signature). Without this signature, it would be impossible to prove the source of transactions propagated on the nodes of the peer-to-peer network. As you can guess, generating and verifying these signatures requires a massive amount of computer power and, since the signatures are complex, their computation may take time thus slowing down the recording of transactions. In comparison, centralized databases (normal ones) do not have to contend with this problem because after the establishment of a connection with the databases, it eliminates the need for individual verification of requests coming over it.

Possible solution: A possible solution for this is the move to proof-of-stake, which would make transactions faster while eliminating the need to have nodes on the network verify individual transactions.

2.   Consensus Mechanism: One of the key characteristic of the blockchain is that it monitors the nodes (computers) on the network and, using some of the computing power of the network, makes sure the nodes within the network reach consensus. Achieving this consensus means there has to be a significant back-and-forth communication between all the nodes and may involve dealing with forks and their effects on the blockchain. This may cause a slowdown of transaction procession. While traditional centralized databases also have to contend with aborted and conflicting transactions, because the database is centralized, these are few.

Possible solution: The consensus mechanism is all about proof-of-work. As the system moves away from proof-of-work to proof-of-stake, it is bound to remove the hindrances that come with it.

The links below detail critical information about the various consensus mechanisms used by various blockchain applications:

https://www.linkedin.com/pulse/types-consensus-mechanism-used-blockchain-munish-singh/

https://bitmalta.com/blockchain-consensus/

3.   Redundancy: In this regard, redundancy does not necessarily mean the performance of individual nodes on the network; it means the amount of computing power required to compute a blockchain. Every node on the blockchain network must process every node individually, something that does not plague centralized databases that process individual transactions just ones. On the blockchain network, this means

more work for the same results, which as you can guess, leads to slowed down processes.

Possible solution: Again, most blockchain application and technologies use proof-of-work to verify transactions. A move to proof-of-stake and other consensus mechanism would eliminate this and take with it the drawbacks.

To learn more about the average time it takes the blockchain network to record transactions, read the insightful content on the links below.

https://coincenter.org/entry/how-long-does-it-take-for-a-bitcoin-transaction-to-be-confirmed

https://bitcoin.stackexchange.com/questions/7323/how-long-does-it-take-on-average-to-receive-one-confirmation-is-it-still-revers

Energy

Many have touted the blockchain technology as the answer to global warming because it provides a transparent currency not based on consumption. Some opine that the innovation as currently instituted — where computer nodes spread across the world have to record all transaction using proof-of-work — leaves a massive carbon imprint because all the computers on the network have to use energy. In fact, some experts are quick to point out that the peer-to-peer power used to process Bitcoins is superior to that of the world's fastest computers combined.

Possible Solution: A possible solution to this is to move away from proof-of-work, thereby eliminating the need for mining, and move to other consensus mechanisms that do not require combined computing power. While this solution may not be forthcoming anytime soon, it shall, and when it does, it shall change everything.

The other solution is a tradeoff between security and size where those spearheading the development of the technology can trade security for size. The downside to this is that the more nodes you have on the network, the more secure it is; however, in an instance where you only want part of the data on the blockchain, perhaps having a smaller, yet faster network would be better. This means that institutions such as banks can set up their smaller blockchain networks and by so doing, save on energy costs, and increase the rate of transaction recording.

Interoperability

Interoperability, making sure that the network and the data therein has standards and is not a bunch of stuff, is a growing concern. Since blockchain technology is open-source and anyone can use it to create whatever blockchain application he or she wants while tweaking it accordingly, there are no set standards for the technology, and competing blockchain platforms are free to use it as they wish. The individual changes and tweaks make it impossible for competing blockchain technologies to achieve a level of interoperability.

Possible solution: A possible solution for this would be for all blockchain-based app developers to achieve consensus and make their individual blockchain applications compatible with the wider web; they can do this by integrating their apps into existing processes and practices.

Privacy

Although most applications using the blockchain technology as their backbone use cryptography to secure data, privacy is a key concern since the blockchain is a publicly visible ledger. This level of openness is not what anyone would consider the most secure way to store sensitive data.

As an example, the Bitcoin blockchain/database has a record of all transactions ever conducted on the platform. This data is open for all to see, which also means anyone can use the same data against someone else. A case in point is the Department of Work and Pension. In May 2016, they started using the blockchain to track how claimants use their benefits.

When you consider that when you conduct transactions over the Bitcoin blockchain, you are publishing your bank statement online for all to see, privacy concerns are sure to arise.

Possible Solution: A possible solution for this would be to use complex cryptographic code to make sure that the transactions are secure and no one can game the system or use the information therein to disadvantage someone else. Another possible solution would be Bitcoin mixing.

The following link has some great ideas on how to enhance privacy over the Bitcoin blockchain (the principles also apply to other blockchain technologies).

https://coinsutra.com/anonymous-bitcoin-transactions/

Changing Truths

The blockchain operates on the premise that all information recorded into it is eternal truth and shall remain so. Reality, as you very well know, is greyer than that. In fact, some jurisdictions such as the EU and the UK have laws detailing the right to be forgotten. For instance, in the UK, if you change your gender, it is your right to have the same reflect all through history (records of birth, baptism, etc.).

If a governmental institution that offers governmental services such as birth records uses a blockchain ledger, that would mean changing such information would be impossible and doing so would lead to the creation of a fork, as was the case with the DAO project.

Encryption

One of the main points we have impressed repeatedly is that most applications on the blockchain technology use cryptography to encrypt information. This encryption creates a number of issues. For one, anyone with a key — perhaps a super user such as the person responsible for creating the specific blockchain application, someone who knows its inner working modalities — can access the encrypted data (so can anyone if the key becomes public). The other issue is that if someone loses the key that unlocks the blockchain, that blockchain would be worthless and difficult, if not impossible to get back.

As the hack on the DAO project proved, encryption, no matter how strong it is, is vulnerable either through the exploitation of backdoors and loopholes, or using new technologies. For instance, even with the immense power of peer-to-peer computing, a technology such as quantum computing (once developed), can knock the bejeezus out of the peer-to-peer network and overpower it, thus making it vulnerable. Therefore, saying we can use cryptography to encrypt the data in the blockchain may not be enough in itself since people will always be looking for ways to de-encrypt encrypted data.

Possible Solution: A possible solution for this would be to make sure that the key that unlocks an encrypted blockchain does not fall into the wrong hands (meaning it should not be public, which in itself presents a problem seeing how the blockchain is an open ledger).

Another solution for this is to implement strong privacy protection laws and strategies. The link below has some invaluable insight into this:

https://github.com/ethereum/wiki/wiki/Problems

Illegal Entries

Consider an instance where someone with malicious intent embeds illegal data into a blockchain. That would make the entire blockchain illegal. It would also mean that anyone on the blockchain would be guilty of breaking the law and therefore culpable.

For instance, James Smith, ODI's Head of Labs Programme and co-author of a report named 'Applying Blockchain Technology in Global Data Infrastructure,' added an illegal encryption key for HD DVD on the PlayStation to the blockchain. To date, no one cares about this and the blockchain upon which the illegal encryption key rests is on everyone's' machine.

Discovering Information

The blockchain database has in place ways to record data (through the computation power of the nodes on the network). However, usage of the data is not as easy since to use the data, you have to find the data you intend to use.

While it is possible to index the blockchain into searchable databases, finding specific information in a reliable manner would require that those participating in the network have the same blockchain history stored on their nodes and a capable search index built from this blockchain. Achieving a distributed search index is something the technology is yet to explore.

Possible solution: A possible solution for information discovery would be to have one site having a search index for the chain. This may lead to possible issues as well since not many would be willing to trust that one site. The lasting solution would be to integrate a capable search feature into the blockchain.

The following links list a number of other blockchain related problems and their possible solutions:

https://appliedblockchain.com/outstanding-challenges-in-blockchain-2017/

https://www.coindesk.com/information/blockchains-issues-limitations/

https://www.kaspersky.com/blog/bitcoin-blockchain-issues/18019/

https://techcrunch.com/2016/02/03/lets-be-honest-about-the-problems-with-blockchain-and-finance/

Now that we have hashed out the possible shortcomings of the blockchain, let us discuss Ethereum, the other blockchain technology that is taking the world by storm and after that, discuss how you can start using the blockchain.

Chapter 10 The Role of Blockchain Technology in Future Capital Markets

Blockchain technology has caused a real stir, particularly in the financial world. Many banks, venture capitalists, and other financial institutions are already looking into how blockchain technology can be used to store data and for other financial uses. One such financial industry is capital markets and it is here that the industry experts are showing the most enthusiasm and optimism about using blockchain technology to solve a number of issues.

Asset Movement

In order for assets to be moved from one financial institution to another, the ledger balances for the assets must also move. This is not an easy job and involves the use of several intermediaries. The more there are involved in the transaction, the more messages need to be exchanged and this results in even more updating of the ledgers required. In an average trade, there are already several intermediaries, including CCPs (central counterparties), exchanges, CSDs (central securities depositories, custodians, brokers and investment managers. In order for the accounting to be correct and for the transaction to be successfully completed, all of the intermediaries involved have to make sure their ledgers are updated based on the messages that are exchanged.

In essence, this means that whenever a transaction takes place, even more messaging needs to be carried out and this causes delays and adds to the total cost. On occasion, in order for a transaction to be completed and all the correct ledger updates made, the intermediaries may have to complete even more ledgers, such as securities borrowing, realignments or cash management. All this does is delay the transaction and is usually referred to, in capital market speak, as a settlement cycle.

So how can blockchain technology help? The creation of a shared flat ledger to process the transactions that happen between several intermediaries is the most important expectation of the capital market industry and will help in cutting both the time and the costs involved in each transaction. Using blockchain technology will also ensure that real-time asset transfers can easily be facilitated.

Financial industries can make use of blockchain technology to build shared flat ledgers that can easily be managed by processing nodes that are trusted. Through the use of digital signatures, the intermediaries will be able to update the ledgers to finish the business transaction. Shared ledgers have to be encrypted so that data confidentiality is maintained. The key processes that are involved in the execution of a trade, like trading, security clearance, settlement and clearing can easily be redesigned and made much simpler with the use of the blockchain.

Onboarding and Maintenance

Account maintenance and client onboarding is the next part of the capital market industry where blockchain technology is highly likely to be put to good use. KYC, or Know Your Customer, costs are incredibly high and cutting down on the cost and cutting out some of the KYC checks that need to be done is just what business the world over are looking to do. If they had a system built in the blockchain that both stored and facilitated Know Your Customer data, they can cut their costs and they can cut down on the amount of YC checks that need to be done. There are already a number of blockchain startup businesses that are focused on the improvement of identity management and we expect to see this number rise significantly over the coming years.

What About Payments?

Payments are a segment of the market where we can expect to see a substantial rise in the use of blockchain technology over the next few years. The blockchain technology can be used to customize the business rules for the processing of transactions, as well as help to tailor these rules to the specific business. This will all be based on the needs of the specific organization and the technology used would be open source software, enabling any number of businesses to use and tailor the software to their own requirements.

Areas that will see the biggest benefits of blockchain technology are bonds trading and OTC (over the counter) derivatives. The technology will be able to provide the business with a secure settlement model that is in real-time and is also cost effective to run, along with being decentralized and global. In short, it really is just a matter of time before the blockchain steps in and starts playing an immense role in capital markets.

A financial services company, based in Belgium and called Euroclear explains how blockchain technology can help the capital market sector. They say that, put basically, the records for every security would be placed onto a flat accounting basis, which means there would be "multiple levels of beneficial ownership" contained on each ledger. There would no more need to operating data normalization for reconciling internal systems or for agreements on exposure and obligation. There would be processes and services that are standardized, reference data would be shared, processing capabilities, like reconciliations, would be standardized, data would be near real-time and there would be a better understanding of the worthiness of counterparts. For regulators and other privileged participants, there would be better transparency on holdings data, along with a whole host of other improvements.

The Benefits for the Capital Market

According to Euroclear, the capital market segment would reap the following benefits:

Pre-Trade

- Better transparency of holdings

- Better verification of holding

- A reduction in credit exposures

- Mutualization of all static data

- Much easier KYC

Trade

- More secure transaction matching in real-time

- Immediate and irrevocable settlement of transactions

- Automatic cash ledger DVP

- Automatic reporting

- Better, more transparent supervision for the market authorities

- Higher standards in AML2

Post-Trade

- Real-time cash transactions do not need to go through central clearing

- Reduced margin requirements

- Reduced collateral requirements

- Interchangeable use of assets as collateral on the blockchain

- Automatic execution of all smart contracts

Securities Servicing and Custody

- Primary proceedings directly to the blockchain

- Automation of servicing processes

- De-duplication of servicing processes

- Better central datasets that have flat accounting orders

- Common data for reference

- Automatic processing of fund subscriptions and redemption directly on the blockchain

- More simplified method of fund servicing

- More simplified method of accounting

- Simpler methods of administration and allocation

Who are the Early Believers and the Pioneers of the Blockchain Technology?

On the Public Platform

1. NASDAQ - In December of 2015, NASDAQ released an official statement to say that Linq, its own blockchain ledger technology, had been successful in completing and recording a private securities transaction. This was the very first time this had been achieved using blockchain. NASDAQ Linq is a digital

ledger that uses the blockchain to aid in the cataloging, issuance and recording of shares that are held in the Private Market by privately held companies. It is designed to complement the cloud-based capitalization management that NASDAQ Private Market, called ExactEquity. Linq clients will be given a full historical and comprehensive record of the issue and transfer of their own securities, providing much better auditability, governance of issue and transfer of ownership.

2.   ASX – the ASX is the largest stock exchange in Australia and it has now confirmed that it is working on the development of a private blockchain in conjunction with Digital Asset, a US-based firm, as a solution for post-trade in the Equity market in Australia. The ASX paid a sum of AUD $14.9 million to gain an equity interest of 5% in Digital Assets Holdings and this fee will be used to fund the first phase of the distributed ledger solution.

On the Private Platform

1.   Chain.com – Chain is a blockchain startup that documents the use of the NASDAQ technology to issue shares to a private investor. The issuer of the securities used NASDAQ Linq to represent, in the digital sense, a record of ownership. The settlement time was reduced significantly and the paper stock certificates were, in effect, redundant. Linq also allows investors and issuers to complete subscription documents and then execute them, all online.

2.   Funderbeam – this company is set to launch the very first investment trading platform that is based on the blockchain technology in the next few months. They will be doing this through a partnership with ChromaWay, a developer of colored coins. Each of the syndicates will be paired up with a micro fund and that micro fund will own real stakes in real startups. As such, when a member of the

syndicate wants to trade some or all of their own holdings, they will actually be trading digital stakes in the micro fund. The blockchain will be used to verify every transaction before it is enforced and the same thing happens when an investor decides to sell all or part of their digital stakes. In each of the investments, the change of ownership will have a distributed audit trail that is fully secure.

The Challenges Faced by the Capital Market in Adopting Blockchain Technology

The capital market will face a number of challenges that they will need to overcome if blockchain technology is to be adopted successfully:

1.   There must be very high standards set for the technology to succeed. This is mainly for the security, for the performance and the robustness of the blockchains. Also, non-blockchain systems, like risk management platforms, will also have to be integrated at some point in the near future.

2.   Legislation and Regulations Must Be Upgraded.   In order for blockchain technologies to be successfully made an integral part of the infrastructure, new regulatory principles will need to be fully integrated.

3.   New Standards and Governance Will Be Required. On some design points, industry alignment will be a requirement. Some of those points include whether the systems in use are fully open, like the bitcoin system, or whether they use a system of permission-based access; the principles that govern whether the system is suitable for interaction with the ledger; whether different systems are interoperable – systems may be running difference safeguards against errors in coding or consensus protocols and this could create knock-on effects that may not be detectable to start with

4.   The Proper Management of the Transition to Minimize Operational Risk. Operational risk is a big consideration and it must be minimized as far as possible.

Blockchain Companies Already Applying Distributed Ledger Security

These companies have already built their systems and are applying the blockchain-based distributed ledger technology to security and compliance

1.   Third-Key Solutions – They provide cryptographic key management solutions and consulting to companies who use distributed blockchains, decentralized digital currencies and asset tokens

2.   Chainalysis – provides products that let financial institutions spot the connections between two or more digital identities and develop lines of trust between them. The products can also help them to identify any malicious actors in the process. Chainalysis states that their mission is to come up with tools that stop any abuse of the system they are being applied to and that respect the privacy of users.

3.   Tradle – uses the blockchain to bridge external and internal financial networks to achieve portability in KYC that is controlled by the user. An open-source mobile framework has been combined with business app development and a full integration platform that allows Tradle to develop sophisticated full-stack blockchain apps

4.   Vogogo – This company specializes in providing verification tools for both payment processing and for risk management. To do this they use a simple JSON REST API.

5.   Elliptic – the first company in the world to secure blockchain asset insurance and to achieve accreditation from

one of the Big Four Audit firms, KPMG. They offer AML bitcoin protection in real-time

6.   Civic – an identity solution that is based on the blockchain, aiming to tackle consumer identity theft and to bring about a reduction in online identity fraud.

7.   Coinalytics – this company allows enterprises to determine real-time risk assessment and intelligence from the decentralized applications and from blockchains. They use methodologies that are based on pattern recognition and on real-time learning online to mine simulated data with few features.

8.   Sig3 – The company uses multi-sig technology to provide extra security layers for transactions made through bitcoin Instead of a requirement for just one signature or one key to make a transaction, the user is able to set up a multi-sig wallet requiring the signature from two of three provided keys before the transaction can be completed and broadcast to the blockchain network. Because Sig3 is an independent automated third-party co-signer, it can be integrated into any multi-sig wallet while maintaining distance from said wallet. This ensures there is no point of failure.

9.   Blockseer - This company has a mission to build a "unified foundation of transparency" for the public ecosystem for bitcoin. By providing the transparency of the blockchain and all of its participants, the company is aiming to cut down on the disorder and chaos and increase knowledge levels and analysis of the public blockchain network

10.   CryptoCorp – This company is a security startup that is focused entirely on bringing about improvements to the bitcoin ecosystem. They offer a service

that is called Digital Oracle, which can take part in multi-signature transactions that originate from any bitcoin wallet

11.	Blockverify – A company that offers an anti-counterfeit system that is based on the blockchain. The system can be applied to luxury items, pharmaceuticals, diamonds and electronics and, using Blockverify, companies will be able to create their own product registers and monitor their own supply chains.

Chapter 11 Building a Mining Rig

Mining Basics

Thousands of computers all over the planet mine cryptocurrencies, and many of these computers are doing so because of viruses designed specifically for mining. If you have ever had your computer slow down because of a virus, it is possible that a miner was installed on your computer.

The reason that someone would design a virus to do disturbed mining is because the component costs to mining are the cost of the hardware and the cost to power the hardware. A virus bypasses both of these costs so that the creator of the virus can only profit. Even so, it is unlikely that the creator of a virus that mines cryptocurrencies has made a tremendous sum of money.

You need very specific hardware to mine cryptocurrencies at an efficient rate. In this chapter you will learn about all of the parts that you will need to build your own mining rig. It might seem like a monumental task, but the truth is that getting a mining rig off the ground is a relatively simple process.

All you need to do is select the parts and build it yourself, or barring that ask for help from a local computer store to help you assemble the parts – this was the avenue I took for my first mining rig, and along with paying for assembly I also paid to learn how to build future rigs by myself.

The key to successful cryptocurrency mining is to buy parts that are power efficient and capable of mining at a fast rate. Since these computers are designed for a singular purpose, there are many standard parts that you will not need. They are also based around desktop parts as these are cheaper, but they also allow for larger graphics processing units (GPU) – the basis for mining efficiently.

The reason that a virus will not be able to mine efficiently, even when on thousands of computers, is that most personal computers today are laptops. Laptops have a central processing unit (CPU) that handles the standard calculations, but also renders all the video and images that you see on your computer monitor.

The fact of the matter is that running calculations on a CPU is incredibly inefficient. A moderately powered graphics card will be able to mine at a far greater rate than even ten or twenty decently powered laptops.

It is important that as you build your mining rig that you spend money on the parts that are important, and minimize the costs on superfluous items. For example, you will not need computer monitors, keyboards and mice or speakers for these computers.

Ideally they do not have more than the parts necessary for efficient mining. You will of course need one monitor and a single keyboard and mouse to set up the mining on machines, but once the setup is complete the rest is handled automatically.

Motherboard

Assembling a modern computer might seem terrifying, but the truth is that it is quite similar to assembling Lego. Each part is a block that plugs into a central board called the 'motherboard'. This base component is where you will put your CPU/GPU and all of the other components that make up your computer. A motherboard is a necessary part, but not one that you should be spending all that much money on.

Even relatively inexpensive motherboards will serve fine for the purposes of mining. The most important aspect is that you buy a motherboard that is full size, as opposed to micro. The main consideration here is heat, and a smaller board does not fare as well as a larger one.

You can expect a motherboard to cost between $50 and $80, with preferable brands being ASUS, GIGABYTE and MSI. What's important is that your motherboard will be a determining factor in the type of central processing unit that you will use.

There are two main suppliers of processors, AMD and Intel. Depending on the motherboard, you will need the corresponding slot type and manufacturer. For example, an Intel LGA1155 board will only take Intel processors of that socket type. Do not let 'LGA1155' scare you – simply put, marketers have not realized the usefulness of catchy names for computer parts.

I strongly urge you to go with an Intel based motherboard capable of fitting an i3 or i5 processor. AMD processors are simply worse at handling heat, which is one of your main concerns for reducing the overhead cost of running a mining rig. You may first want to look at your choices of CPU and then base your motherboard decision off of what processor you will be purchasing.

As a general rule of thumb, processor costs are more fixed than motherboards. You may find an excellent sale on a motherboard, but it unlikely that the cost of a processor will change. Typically the manufacturer of CPUs will issue parts and never adjust the prices, only modifying pricing when new models of processors come out.

You should note that a motherboard will have many components already built into it. For example, your networking capability should be built into your motherboard. This is where you will also find your audio outputs and inputs for keyboard and mouse.

Power Supply

The power supply is the most important component of a mining rig. I have heard countless stories of people buying a cheap power supply only to see their mining rig burst into flames. This is not meant to be alarmist – power supplies are very safe, but they range in build quality greater than any other part on this list. The power supply is so essential because the computer will be running twenty-four hours a day, so stability is key.

I would recommend an EVGA, Thermaltake, or CORSAIR power supply. They come in different wattages, but for your needs, you must simply look for one that is 400 watts or greater. You should also note that power supplies are graded in terms of quality. Provided you buy a power supply that is silver or gold rated, you will be fine.

Additionally, the manufactures I have listed only make high quality power supplies, so even a bronze rated EVGA power supply will be sufficient. Expect the cost of a power supply to range between $50 and $80, depending on sales and promotions.

Power supplies should be changed out every eighteen months. All power supplies fail; the question is merely a matter of time, and how they will die. A poorly manufactured power supply will take all of the connected parts with it, meaning that an entire rig can be lost. A well-made power supply will simply stop working, meaning you can salvage all of the parts in the machine. You would simply need to replace the power supply to get it running again.

Since these machines are running at maximum load all of the time, an eighteen month period of use is to be expected. You can run them for longer, but you always risk a failure that may take out other parts with it.

Graphics Card (GPU)

The graphics card is the second most important part of your mining rig. This is where the true computational power comes into play. While a central processing unit can only handle a few calculations at a time, a graphics card can handle hundreds at the same time. It is a byproduct of their design, taking instructions from the CPU to power onscreen images. The relative power in each core of the GPU is low, but with so many of them they can mine much more efficiently than any CPU.

There are two main brands to buy from for graphics processors, NVidia and AMD. This is the same AMD that also makes CPUs, and for what it is worth the other main CPU manufacturer, Intel, owns NVidia. Both companies have good models of consumer video cards for mining. Most recently both companies have released new products that consume less power and are more efficient when it comes to heat.

There is a bit of a trade off in these two manufacturers. NVidia costs a bit more, and is not as fast as similar AMD cards, however they are more reliable overall, consume less power and produce drastically less heat. For my own rigs, I primarily use NVidia cards. This is merely because their cards were available to me before the latest line of AMD cards.

I would recommend that you either use a NVidia 1060 ($250) or an AMD 480 ($200). Both of these models have variations depending on the manufacturer of the card. For example you may see an EVGA 480, but this is the same base product as the one that AMD offers.

Without getting into too many details, the boards are free to be manufactured provided the companies get royalties for the technology. The primary difference is sometimes the clock speeds are increased, or the mounted cooling units are more efficient. There is no brand of either GPU that I would not recommend, and in fact I would just go with whatever is cheapest.

In these various models you will also see that they are differentiated based on the amount of memory that they have, coming in 3 and 6 GB versions for NVidia, and 4 and 8 GB versions for AMD. For the purposes of mining, the onboard video memory does not matter – buy the card with less memory as it will always be cheaper.

A GPU should be replaced once every two to three years, but the main catalyst for replacement should be that a new and more efficient model has been released. When a GPU dies, it simply stops working, so the build quality is not as essential as with a power supply.

It is my recommendation that if you start building mining rigs, you on occasion look at benchmarks for power efficiency in video cards. New cards come out roughly every year or so, with major revisions happening every two to four years – the latest major revisions were in 2016.

Central Processing Unit (CPU)

For processors you have a choice between Intel and AMD. What processor type you buy does not matter that much, as both are equally suitable for mining. What is important is that the socket type of the processor matches the motherboard that you buy. With this, it is my advice that you buy your motherboard and CPU at the same time, if only to ensure compatibility.

Like with video cards, the differences between the types of CPUs come down to heat and cost. AMD costs less but produces more heat. Intel costs more but produces less heat. Remember that more heat means more power consumption, and so you can trade the upfront cost for long term savings by going with Intel, or you can pay less now and go with AMD.

This is one of the more expensive parts of a mining rig, with the average cost of a processor being slightly over $200. The naming convention of the AMD processors is not as intuitive as the Intel system. I would suggest an i3 processor for Intel, which could cost as low as $150, or any AMD processor that is 'Bulldozer' or newer.

The upper limit for the cost of this part is $250, with the cheapest processor type coming in at $150. Other guides may suggest going with an i5 Intel processor, but the truth is that you don't really need this type of power. We are building a mining rig for home use, not a rig that will be joined with hundreds of other computers in a warehouse.

Memory (RAM)

The random access memory, or RAM, is a part that should not cost you more than $40 or $50. There are many different manufacturers of RAM, and I cannot recommend one brand over any other; that is because there is a consistent quality to RAM, which has more or less made it a commodity. You will need between 4 and 8 GB of system ram for efficient mining. 4 GB is fine in 2017, but by 2018 or 2019 you will likely want to have 8GB of RAM in your system.

This is an easily upgradeable part, so I would buy the cheapest and smallest amount as you get started. Please note that while the numbers and markings are the same, system RAM is very different from video card memory. One does not substitute the other, so even if you have a 3 GB video card, you will still need 4 GB of system RAM for your rig.

Storage

Storage is an essential part of any computer, but not one that you should spend a lot of money on. Storage options come in the form of hard drives (HDD) and solid state drives (SSD), with the latter being far more expensive. There has been a push for miners to move to SSD due to the lower power usage, but I have found the cost of SSDs to be so great that the upfront cost does not justify the long term power usage.

Any hard drive from any manufacturer will do – look for storage sizes of 80 GB up to 1 TB, and buy whatever part is cheapest. Note that hard drives do fail and that without a storage drive your rig will stop working. You will need to replace it if it fails, but you will not lose any of your cryptocurrency, as that is stored on the public ledger and not locally on your machine.

Operating System

Your options for operating systems are Windows or Linux, and I highly recommend the later. A Linux license is free and an image can be found online quite easily. To install an operating system like Linux, simply create a bootable flash drive by following the instructions provided by the specific version of Linux that you install. I would recommend Linux Red Hat or Ubuntu – you can think of these naming conventions as Windows 7, 10 etc.

They all have the same foundation but their interface is slightly different. Before you decide on the version of Linux that you want, I do suggest that you look at a compatibility chart to ensure your preferred cryptocurrency is listed. Once you have Linux installed, you must simply download the cryptocurrency client that you wish to mine. Install the client, set up an account and follow the instructions to start mining.

Chapter 12 Blockchain Technology Myths

It is very clear that the technology behind the blockchain is going to be the most important computing invention of this generation. This is because, for the very first time in the history of the human being, we have a full digital exchange for peer-to-peer value. Blockchain is a massive global platform and is firmly based on distributed ledger. It is responsible for establishing the rules, in the format of very heavy encryption and computations, that let at least two parties carry out transactions without the need for a centralized third party agency involved to establish the trust between the parties.

Instead of being reliant on government agencies, banks or any other intermediary to create that trust, the technology that fuels the blockchain ensures that trust is provided through clever doing and collaboration on a mass scale. The trust is actually built into the blockchain system and that is why the blockchain is otherwise known as "The Trust Protocol".

If we wanted to take that a step further, the blockchain plays several other roles. It is:

- An accounts ledger

- A database

- A sentry

- A clearing house

It is, in all likelihood, going to be the second-generation internet and it has the potential to take the economic grid and rewire it to run things for the better, shaking up the old and bringing in a completely new way of working. A fresh perspective on old business systems.

Sadly, there are still a lot of myths about blockchain technology doing the rounds and these are responsible for putting a lot of influential businesses and people off of using it. Here are the top 5 of those blockchain myths, busted and explained:

1.   Blockchain is good but bitcoin is bad

There are an awful lot of people, particularly in the financial sector that are very excited about the potential that blockchain technology provides. However, those same people are under the misconception that digital currencies are not feasible, they are not desirable and are in fact quite dangerous.

The blockchain for bitcoin is a permission less system, which means that anyone is able to get into it through a device that has internet access and can interact with it in the same way they do the internet. Blockchains that are permissioned, on the other hand, require that all users have specific credentials, such as an operator's license for the blockchain they want to access, and those credentials are provided by a governing body or by the members of the blockchain. These permissioned systems use the distributed ledger technology but do not have any digital currency attached to them.

At first look, the permissioned or private blockchain looks like having several advantages. For a start, members of the chain are able to make changes to the rules if they want to. They are only required to get the group they are a part of to agree to make the change, rather than having to get an entire network involved. Costs are reduced because the transactions only have to be validated by the chain members, not by that massive network. All of this can also help reduce the costs of electricity, benefitting the environments and regulators are likely to prefer them over and over the public chain, like bitcoin, because there is no need to anonymity.

But, there are some things to consider. If it is easy to change rules, it is easy to flaunt those same rules. When you limit freedoms intentionally, neutrality can be severely inhibited. If the open value innovation goes, the blockchain technology will do nothing more than stagnate and vulnerabilities will open up in it. The bitcoin blockchain, on the other hand, and any other that is tied to digital currencies, include incentives built in to encourage users to validate the transactions.

2.   The financial services are the only real industry that will benefit from blockchains

Provided they are able to locate the right leadership, the FSI can alter itself using the technology behind blockchain. That technology has the potential to completely revolutionize financial services, from the humble bank account and debit card right up to the entire credit card network. If everyone is sharing the same distributed ledger, transaction settlements can happen straight away for everyone. Banks could use blockchain technology to speed up the system process and reduce the massive costs they face every day. The smartest of them will strategically use the technology, and that includes the permission less system, to get into newer markets and bring a whole bunch of new services out.

But the FSI is only a small part of the whole system. Blockchains have the potential to disrupt those that are already seen as the disrupters, like Uber. Blockchains will be at the very center of the IoT (Internet of Things) and will allow the smart device to contract with, carry out transactions and share data securely peer-to-peer.

The blockchain has the potential to completely reinvent how democracy works by ensuring that politicians have to do something they are not used to doing – be accountable to the public.

3.   Blockchains are B2B (business to business) and not for the general public

So many people are convinced that blockchain technology will turn around the economy and shake up our day to day life in more ways than we could imagine. They are not just for businesses, as others believe; the blockchain will have an effect on every man, woman and child in the world today.

4.   There are too many issues with blockchains to make them work

There are those who say that blockchain technology really isn't ready for the world yet. It's too difficult to use properly and the best applications are still growing, still being developed. There are others who say that there is a huge amount of energy required to get consensus across the network. They ask what would happen when millions of blockchains all connected, are processing untold numbers of transactions every day. Are there sufficient incentives in place to get people to take part and not try to overthrow the entire network? Could blockchain possibly be the biggest killer of jobs for people of all time? Instead of seeing these are bad reasons for taking on the technology, we should perhaps be looking at them as challenges of implementing the system.

5.   Satoshi Nakamoto is actually Craig Wright

Craig Wright is an Australian entrepreneur who has sensationally claimed that he is the original inventor of the bitcoin, Satoshi Nakamoto. We already know that Satoshi is the only creator; there were others involved. When the first bitcoin paper was written, and the first protocol, that was what got things started. Then that person disappeared off the scene, leaving the community to keep the work going. It is that community that is responsible for most of the blockchain code and all other bitcoin-related content. In that case, everyone in the community is actually Satoshi.

This is why it doesn't really matter who the original protocol. It is a permission less system and that means there will never be an arbitrator. For the next step to be taken, the entire community has to be the governor for things to move forward. The likelihood of Craig Wright being the real Satoshi Nakamoto is very slim though

Conclusion

There is little doubt that blockchain technology will greatly change the global economy in coming years. From revamping the way that information is shared across organizations, to possibly being the underlying technology for a government issued cryptocurrency, the strength of blockchain lies in its ability to force cooperation among many disparate parties.

You are now well aware of where the future is heading, and what you can expect from the future of blockchain technology. You also have a firm understanding of how cryptocurrencies work, and how you can make a profit by mining them yourself.

I compiled the material in this book based on a single idea, for the reader to educate him or herself on blockchain and to make an impact on that reader's life. I hope that you feel enlightened about the nature of blockchain, and that you find some of the same amazement that I have over the years, about the genius of its creation and the interesting nature of its creators. It is truly an invention of the Internet era; a technology to restore power to the people.

By spreading information without a central institution or authority, blockchain democratizes information in much the same way the Internet originally did. It serves as a platform for services, ranging from databases to currencies, but its uses will grow far greater than anything we have seen in its current form today.

The last chapter of this book is dedicated to the idea of mining cryptocurrencies for profit. I know that for some readers this idea will seem fanciful, as if it is reserved for only the most technically inclined. I want to assure you that the only thing necessary to mine cryptocurrencies is the motivation and desire for profit. I came to blockchain technology purely out of fascination, but as I learned and started to understand how blockchain works, I have found that mining is a simple process that can be used to supplement your income.

I urge you to consider building your own mining rig; the cost of investment is low, and the potential for profit is unlimited. A mining rig is a platform to generate profit for many years into the future. While it is true that the exact amount of profit is unknown, cryptocurrencies have proven to be overall resilient enough that they are worth the investment.

Thank you and good luck!

The World of Cryptocurrency:

A Guide to Understanding the Highly Profitable Investing of Digital Currency and its Future Potential

David Vela

Table of Contents

Introduction

The term cryptocurrency is used to define a form of virtual currency that can only be purchased and traded online. These currencies are completely independent of any government entity and therefore represent unregulated, unmonitored and untraceable ways to transfer funds instantly and with zero fees.

Cryptocurrencies have garnered a lot of public attention in recent years due to the vast financial successes obtained by investors. Just like any other currency or stock, the value of cryptocurrencies fluctuates based on market demand & supply. However, the trade of these currencies remains unregulated by any government entity and therefore often exhibits unique behaviors that are not commonly seen in FIAT currencies (Dollar, Euro, CAD, Japanese Yen, Chinese Yuan, and so on).

For instance, it is highly unlikely that a FIAT currency such as the US Dollar fluctuates in value by 5 percentage points throughout the course of a single day. However, it is not rare for cryptocurrencies to experience daily fluctuations of over 20%. To the unaware, unexperienced investors these price variations represent a hurdle or an obstacle. But to the uncanny and experienced investor these fluctuations in value represent opportunity – the opportunity to make 20% return in a single day!

Those of you who possess a fundamental understanding in the field of economics are probably raising their brows in skepticism and wondering: "the value of any currency must be backed by a real-world asset in order to be recognized, what on earth could cryptocurrencies be backed by?"

For instance, the US dollar was backed by gold and silver until 1971. Now it is only backed by "government debt" – this means the government vows to accept dollar bills in exchange for goods and services and will enforce this system with the law. Let's return to the subject of our book now and focus on the question at hand: "what is cryptocurrency backed by?"

This may seem a tricky question – cryptocurrencies cannot be exchanged for goods or services like the US Dollar, they do not even exist in physical form! So, what can you use them for? Any cryptocurrency can be used for one thing and one only: gaining access to the Blockchain Platform. The power and capabilities of this platform determine the value of each cryptocurrency, this is what cryptocurrencies are backed by: not gold, not silver, not a government system, but by their Blockchain platform. Now you will find yourself asking: "what is a Blockchain platform?"

These platforms are new and revolutionary computer infrastructures that offer incredible advantages in terms of database storage and computational speed to large companies. To put this into perspective, it is estimated that Blockchain technology will reduce infrastructure costs of major US investment banks by about 12 billion dollars before 2025. Please appreciate the massive numbers we are dealing with in this subject – the growth potential for the future is immense.

When a smart, well-informed investors finds a large market and high growth potential he immediately recognizes an opportunity – in this book I want to show you how to grab this opportunity. In the first chapters I will provide you with a fundamental understanding of cryptocurrencies and the role of Blockchain technology in today's market.

After covering the fundamental background knowledge, we will dive into real hands-on experience. I will show you how to purchase cryptocurrencies using today's most effective online Exchange platforms and how to store them securely and safely using an eWallet. Finally, in the last section of the book I will discuss the future of the market. In this section I will show you how to evaluate the potential of a new cryptocurrency and what investment strategies you can employ to achieve the highest returns.

Please understand this book will not make you an expert trader in cryptocurrencies. I challenge any single book to make this claim – today's cryptocurrency market is a new and extremely complicated space that is constantly evolving and reshaping in unexpected ways. There are still many unexplored paths and a vast amount of concepts to prove.

The purpose of this guide is very different – I want to provide you with a fundamental understanding of the underlying technology and show you where to purchase, store and sell your first virtual coins! Essentially, I want to show you how to get started quickly and effectively.

Thanks for downloading this book. It's my firm belief that it will provide you with all the answers to your questions.

Chapter 13 Cryptocurrencies Explained

For thousands and thousands of years, barter was the way of things. Currencies were essentially whatever was on hand that could be easily traded to other interested parties who were nearby and amiable to the process. Eventually, urbanization and modernization resulted in the creation of currencies that took the place of barter and enabled an easier form of trade across larger distances. The creation of the internet enabled transactions across even vaster distances with individuals exchanging currencies for goods and services worldwide in a way that our ancestors could never have imagined.

To go along with this most recent expansion, cryptocurrencies have been created which are a purely digital medium of exchange that is based on computer code instead of hard assets and relies purely on the market to determine exchange rates and to monitor the creation of new units. Cryptocurrencies offer an alternative that has proven surprisingly viable when compared to physical currency over the past decade. They offer value in a purely digital sense and concerns when it comes to issuing and tracking are all dealt with in a purely digital space.

Cryptocurrencies are entirely self-contained in that they offer autonomous control and tracking of each unit of currency, often without any type of governing body whatsoever. Bitcoin is by far the most famous example but there are currently more than a thousand types of cryptocurrencies all vying for dominance in the virtual market. Each has unique strengths and weakness and it is likely that one of these will eventually dethrone bitcoin as the cryptocurrency of choice simply because it has been built on bitcoin's strengths while possessing none of its weaknesses. Current contenders for the throne include ether which allows for easier interface with a wide variety of virtual machines and is primarily used to pay for services while also interacting more smoothly with smart contracts and litecoin whose main claim to fame is that it offers much faster confirmation times than bitcoin.

Unlike more traditional currencies there is no true limit on what a single unit of cryptocurrency could be worth with some currently being valued at 1 cent and others, such as bitcoin, currently being valued at over $2,000. Cryptocurrencies currently come in two forms, those that are controlled from a single source in a centralized fashion or those, like bitcoin, that are purely controlled by the market. Decentralized cryptocurrencies utilize a variety of different verification methods when it comes to ensuring transactions get where they need to go. The most common of these is a proof-of-work verification process which is frequently referred to as mining though options such as consensus protocols and consensus platforms are also used in some cases.

Pricing

Due to the fact that there are no government bodies watching over cryptocurrency prices, these currencies must maintain their prices using different methods. Cryptocurrency price is a reflection of its value to the market, just as with any other currency type which means demand is the core determining factor when it comes to price, they just have fewer restrictions holding them back when compared to more standard models.

External factors also play a bigger role in cryptocurrencies than they do in traditional currencies, simply due to the fact that there are fewer filters between these forces and the market that drives them. Those who spend their days trading cryptocurrencies also often play a measurable role in the determination of price, especially among the smaller types of cryptocurrency. Cryptocurrency traders work just like any other type of trader in that they purchase a given currency and hold onto for a varying length of time in hopes that the price will rise and they will profit from their investment. If enough individuals purchase and hold onto a specific currency then they can conspire to drive the price to levels that are higher than demand and general usefulness otherwise would.

While it is sometimes positive, for those holding the currency at least, outside influences can also be negative, driving the price down despite its usefulness and demand remaining relatively stable. When this occurs, the creators of these currencies often step in and attempt to utilize additional outside forces as a means of countering downward trends. The ways in which they do so are discussed below.

Media: Media coverage, regardless of the media in question, is one of the main ways that those on the fringes of the cryptocurrency world often decide which cryptocurrency to focus on at a given time. Increased public interest then naturally leads to an increase in price. The media often gets involved primarily when a new cryptocurrency starts showing up on cryptocurrency exchanges or when a cryptocurrency that has already been publicized previously receives a major code update by its developers. Additional media worthy events include anything that can be compressed into a soundbite in such a way that it proves the cryptocurrency is currently growing in popularity and has an active community surrounding it. Virtually any type of media coverage is going to affect the price in a positive way.

Public opinion: As with anything else online, even the most obscure type of cryptocurrency likely has a rabid fanbase that is at the vanguard when it comes to trying to convince others that their choice of cryptocurrency is the right one. These individuals are extremely useful when it comes to inflating the price of the cryptocurrency in question as the more publicized faith it has, the more likely that other people are going to be willing to invest money in it. Additionally, these vanguards provide valuable feedback to developers, tinker with the opensource code and also invest their own funds, thus driving the price even higher.

The best example of this core-user snowball effect happened with the bitcoin bubble of 2014. Bitcoin slowly grew in price and use for the first five years of its existence. Then, the number of users hit a tipping point and suddenly, a currency that was once previously worth less than a dollar per coin was suddenly propelled to prices over $1,000. This is when serious investors started to take notice and the price has, more or less, never looked back.

Bots: As with any asset, liquidity is the key to growth for any cryptocurrency. Unlike with other types of assets, if a given cryptocurrency is not growing at a rate that major investors are looking for they can increase its relative level of liquidity by employing bots to work the market and get things moving in the desired direction. Liquidity refers to the amount of a given asset that is currently available for trade and if liquidity is low then those looking to trade a given cryptocurrency won't be able to buy it. As such, bots are employed to buy and sell the cryptocurrency in question, stimulating growth of that specific economy which causes additional units of the currency to be produced and liquidity to improve. China, which has very few restrictions on its bitcoin exchanges compared to the rest of the world, is frequently credited with a vast amount of this type of trading and is thus responsible for much of bitcoin's liquidity.

Social media: Unlike more traditional currencies where news spreads through more traditional channels, a majority of the information regarding upcoming changes in cryptocurrency policy breaks via social media. There are countless groups across all platforms dedicated to cryptocurrency and the followers of each are generally rabid in their fervor for the cause. Due to their enthusiasm, it only takes a small positive mention of a given cryptocurrency for these followers to jump on a given bandwagon.

This has caused a unique phenomenon where those with a vested interest in a given cryptocurrency have taken to spreading false positive rumors as a means of artificially inflating prices, at least until the rumor is proven unfounded. Even then, if the rumor was relating to a potential incoming price increase then it is often a self-fulfilling prophecy as the rumor of a price increase often leads to a run on the currency in question which then creates the price increase that the rumor was trying to achieve.

Pump and dump: This type of influencing currency isn't limited to just the cryptocurrency space as those with a vested interest have been guilty of doing it for years. The only real difference is that it isn't illegal with cryptocurrencies and is instead just frowned upon by those in the market that is affected. The basis of the pump and dump is that the initiating party purchases as much of the cryptocurrency in question as possible, limiting the available stock as much as possible over an extended period of time. The market then responds to this shortage by increasing the price in response to the perceived demand.

In the cryptocurrency space, exchanges operate via what are known as digital order books which list all of the trades made for a specific cryptocurrency over a specific period of time. If the order books are empty of those looking to sell, the price naturally increases to combat the scarcity. Once this occurs, those who bought up all the available stock of cryptocurrency can then sell, making a tremendous profit in the process.

Once the pump has been successful, the next phase, the dump, occurs as the holder of all of the currency releases it all back onto the market at once, sending prices rocketing back in the other direction.

Chapter 14 Types of cryptocurrencies

While bitcoin is the most well-known cryptocurrency these days, it is far from the only game in town. What follows are a few of the major types of cryptocurrency on the market these days that bear keeping a closer eye on. This is only a brief overview, however, as not only are the specifics of these cryptocurrencies in a constant state of flux, new and relevant forms of cryptocurrency are always arriving on the scene. All of these coins are available for purchase on most currently active cryptocurrency exchanges.

Ether: Ether is the currency of the Ethereum network and it primarily exchanged for services related to distributed applications and smart contracts. Ether is used to run the virtual machines that run these applications which rely on gas, or a portion of a single ether, in order to cover their operating costs to the system as a whole. Roughly 18 million new ether are created every year.

Ether is noteworthy because before the end of 2017 it will switch from a proof-of-work validation system to what is known as a proof-of-stake validation system. Unlike with the standard blockchain model, this validation system works by choosing the creator of the next block in a partially random way and the chance that a specific account will be chosen is defined by the amount of ether in that account. Blocks will then be said to be forged instead of mined. Forgers will receive transaction fees but not traditional mining rewards.

In early 2017, a variety of research groups, Fortune 500 companies and blockchain startups, more than one hundred in all, formed the Ethereum Alliance which is a nonprofit organization whose purpose is to engineer an open-source standard as well as a private version of the Ethereum blockchain that will be able to address the interests of a variety of industries from, banking to healthcare, in a more practical way.

In the Ethereum blockchain, smart contracts are stored publicly on every node in the blockchain. This means that performance issues sometimes arise as every node is calculating a given smart contract at the same time which leads to lower speeds. The Ethereum blockchain can process about 25 transactions per second currently but greater scalability is possible. As of July 2017, a single ether is worth about $196.46.

Litecoin: Litecoin is, in many respects, very similar to bitcoin, though it features some technical improvements as well. It allows for a much greater number of transactions to be processed over a shorter period of time which prevents the bottlenecks that are seen with bitcoin today. Its blocks are processed in approximately two and a half minutes as compared to bitcoin's ten-minute limit. This can lead to a higher number of orphaned blocks, however, though it also leads to a decreased chance of a double spending attack occurring. Overall, it requires approximately ten times less work from a computational standpoint to mine a litecoin block than a bitcoin block. It also offers very low payments costs and completes payments approximately four times faster than bitcoin does.

The Litecoin Network is currently working to produce eighty-four million litecoins which is four times the number of bitcoins currently in circulation. As of July 2017, a single litecoin is worth about $41.30.

Dogecoin: The dogecoin features a likeness of the Siba Inu dog from the doge internet meme that was extremely popular in 2013. Due to a successful crowdfunding campaign, a solid gold dodgecoin is on track to be sent to the moon in 2019. While it was first introduced as somewhat of a joke, hence the meme logo, it rapidly developed an online following and reached a capitalization of greater than $60 million in less than a month. What sets it apart from other cryptocurrencies is its rapid coin production schedule and in its first year and a half 100 million coins were produced. It is most commonly uses as a means for social media users to tip one another when particularly noteworthy content is provided.

Dogecoin offers a one-minute processing time and there is no limit to how many can ultimately be produced. Currently 5.26 billion dogecoins are produced per year. As of July 2017, a single dogecoin is worth approximately $1,255.

Chapter 15 Examples of Cryptocurrency

Are you starting to get a clearer picture about cryptocurrency? One thing you would have probably realized by now is that it is in no way a simple concept. Cryptocurrency comes with a lot of information and consideration in order for someone to really, profoundly understand it.

Read on to learn more about how to buy and use it, a few of the most popular examples of it and a few of the most common terms you'd be encountering when dealing with it.

Some Examples of Cryptocurrency

In order to give you an even better picture of the kinds of cryptocurrency, let's take a look at the most popular and most widely used kinds of cryptocurrencies which are currently available in the market now.

Knowing these would at least give you an idea on what cryptocurrencies are out there and which ones you can start researching on more.

• Bitcoin

The very first and most well known cryptocurrency. Even if you haven't started using cryptocurrency, you've probably already heard of this. Bitcoin acts as the digital standard for gold in the entire industry of cryptocurrency. It is widely used as a global method of payment and is the actual currency used in most cyber crimes such as in ransomware or in the darknet market.

Since it was released in 2009, the price of Bitcoin has then gone up from zero to more than $650 million. The volume of transactions has already reached more than 200,000 transactions on a daily basis. Because of this, it looks like Bitcoin has good sustainability.

- Ethereum

Created by Vitalik Buterin, a crypto-genius, this kind of cryptocurrency has rapidly grown in popularity, second to Bitcoin.

It has a blockchain technology is able to balance and validate accounts and process transactions but it is also able to process intricate programs and contracts as well.

There are different versions of Ethereum, thus making it more of a group of currencies rather than an individual kind of currency.

- Litecoin

Litecoin happens to be one of the first cryptocurrencies that was created after Bitcoin. It is known as the "silver" to the "digital gold" Bitcoin.

This is much quicker, has a bigger quantity of tokens and has a newer mining algorithm. This innovation had seemed to be perfectly customized to be like a smaller version of Bitcoin. Through it, or rather through the basecode used in it, other similar cryptocurrencies (such as Feathercoin and Dogecoin) came into being.

Though it has lost its second place standing after Bitcoin, it is still being actively cultivated and users still use it for trading now.

- Monero

Monero is probable the best model which makes use of the cryptonite algorithm, which was created to add some useful features in terms of privacy.

Unlike with Bitcoin and other cryptocurrencies where each transaction is recorded in the blockchain technology, Monero had a feature known as ring-signatures. This is the cryptonite algorithm which severed the trail of transaction records, granting users a higher degree of privacy.

In the year 2016, Monero reached its peak because the darknet markets made the decision to use it as their currency. Because of this, the price had gone higher, however, the actual utilization of this particular cryptocurrency remains lesser.

- Blackcoin

To be able to verify a Blackcoin block, the user must stake a number of coins from their own waller as PoS. Coins are spent if the block isn't confirmed.

In Blackcoins, the mining process is a lot faster and it doesn't consume as much power.

- Dash

Anonymity is the main feature of this kind of cryptocurrency as it makes use of "Masternodes" in completing transactions.

Wish Dash, it is difficult, if not impossible for other users to view your savings or any of your transactions as it doesn't have a public ledger.

- Dogecoin

The Hash Algorithm Scrypt was created through this particular cryptocurrency. This was supposed to avoid the monopolization of mining by a single person or huge organizations.

Though the system didn't actually work, a lot of people still choose to use Dogecoin.

- Peercoin

This cryptocurrency is different from others as it has a PoS / PoW fusion feature. There is no bound on the number of coins mined however it was created to ultimately get an inflation rate of 1%

- Ripple

However less popular (some even say this is the most hated one), it would be helpful to learn about this particular kind of cryptocurrency too.

While Ripple has its own local cryptocurrency (which is the XRP), it is more like a network which is used to process IOUs rather than the actual cryptocurrency itself.

The local currency doesn't actually work as a means to store and exchange value but more as something for the network to use as protection from spam.

Because of this, users don't consider Ripple as a real cryptocurrency as it doesn't have respectable store value.

Aside from these most well-known cryptocurrencies, there are hundreds more. Some are more reputable than others while some are merely attempts to make a quick buck or to get the attention of investors.

Again, be sure to do enough research on the kinds of cryptocurrencies before deciding on which to go with. We will be talking about other kinds further on so keep on reading!

Chapter 16 Useful Terms You May Encounter

To be able to gain a full understanding of cryptocurrency and everything it comprises, it would also be useful to learn the most common terms used when dealing with it. To avoid confusion and to be able to keep up with the trend, you need to have an idea of these terms and what they mean.

Being able to understand technical terms in any concept is useful, and learning about cryptocurrency is no different. Build your cryptocurrency knowledge bank by familiarizing yourself with these terminologies.

1. 51% Attack

This is the name given to a condition wherein more than 50% of the computing authority in a network is controlled by just one person or a single group. This authority then gives them full and total rule over the network.

2. Address

This is the location where you would hold, send or receive your cryptocurrency. On the other hand, a wallet address is the public part of the keys needed for you to go through with your transactions.

3. Altcoin

This is the most accepted name for any cryptocurrency which isn't Bitcoin.

4. ASIC or ASIC Miner

ASIC (which means application-specific integrated circuit) mining is a cunning way to mine different coins at a quicker rate. An ASIC is basically a chip which is purposely made for mining. So an ASIC miner is someone who works on mining using this chip.

5. Blockchain

Already mentioned a couple of times in this book, a blockchain is a data system which permits the formation of a documentation of all the transactions made in a network which isn't centralized.

Through cryptography, people and computers around the globe are able to work together to be able to design a network as opposed to a network being designed or created by a single person or group. As a plus, the network is also protected by the cryptography.

Now the blockchain is made up of blocks made by people and it constantly grows as each block is created. Another feature of a blockchain is that it can be seen by everyone.

d6. Block

These are files in a digital documentation. Data on these blocks cannot be modified and they are permanently stored once they are verified.

7. Block Height

This refers to the quantity of blocks following the first block in a blockchain.

8. Block Reward

This is the incentive given to a miner when he/she is able to successfully hash or solve a mathematical problem in regards to a block.

9. Central and Distributed Ledger

A central ledger is a written arrangement of synchronized data which is replicable but is managed by a single person or network.

A distributed ledger is a written arrangement of shared, synchronized data which can be replicated and therefore spread throughout different networks through different computers.

10. Fork

This refers to the enduring deviation of a different working version of the blockchain. These usually emerge when there is a 51% attack, a bug is found in the program or new rules would surface.

11. Halving

This is the decrease of minable rewards after a certain number of blocks have been created.

12. Hashrate

This refers to the rate at which a block is uncovered as well as the rate at which a mathematical problem which is related to it is solved.

13. Mining

This refers to the process of discovering and solving blocks on a blockchain.

14. Multisig

This refers to a form of security wherein there is more than just one signature to grant a transaction and this is very useful in business setting.

15. Node

This is basically a computer which is linked to the network. It serves as a support for the network through the process of relaying and validating transactions while being able to obtain a duplicate of the entire blockchain.

16. P2P

A shortcut of the term peer-to-peer. Interactions in a blockchain can be done through P2P.

17. PoW

This means Proof of Work. It was originally created to prevent DDOS attacks and spam emails. This is basically date which is extremely expensive to make however it can be easily confirmed by another party.

18. PoS

This means Proos of Stake. It is considered as the better substitute for PoW. The difference is that this system demands to be shown evidence of ownership of a certain amount of money.

19. Public and Private Key

This is a term used in cryptography and it refers to the key which can be used to encrypt and decode a message.

20. Signature

This is a mathematical equation which is used to test someone to prove that they, in fact, own the data, wallet or such.

21. Smart Contract

This is an agreement kept within a blockchain which cannot be modified. It has specific operations based on logic and is similar to written contracts.

These are the most common terminologies you would be able to encounter when dealing with cryptocurrency. Now that you know them, you would be more familiar when you decide to start using them.

Chapter 17 Building a Mining Rig

Mining Basics

Thousands of computers all over the planet mine cryptocurrencies, and many of these computers are doing so because of viruses designed specifically for mining. If you have ever had your computer slow down because of a virus, it is possible that a miner was installed on your computer.

The reason that someone would design a virus to do disturbed mining is because the component costs to mining are the cost of the hardware and the cost to power the hardware. A virus bypasses both of these costs so that the creator of the virus can only profit. Even so, it is unlikely that the creator of a virus that mines cryptocurrencies has made a tremendous sum of money.

You need very specific hardware to mine cryptocurrencies at an efficient rate. In this chapter you will learn about all of the parts that you will need to build your own mining rig. It might seem like a monumental task, but the truth is that getting a mining rig off the ground is a relatively simple process.

All you need to do is select the parts and build it yourself, or barring that ask for help from a local computer store to help you assemble the parts – this was the avenue I took for my first mining rig, and along with paying for assembly I also paid to learn how to build future rigs by myself.

The key to successful cryptocurrency mining is to buy parts that are power efficient and capable of mining at a fast rate. Since these computers are designed for a singular purpose, there are many standard parts that you will not need. They are also based around desktop parts as these are cheaper, but they also allow for larger graphics processing units (GPU) – the basis for mining efficiently.

The reason that a virus will not be able to mine efficiently, even when on thousands of computers, is that most personal computers today are laptops. Laptops have a central processing unit (CPU) that handles the standard calculations, but also renders all the video and images that you see on your computer monitor.

The fact of the matter is that running calculations on a CPU is incredibly inefficient. A moderately powered graphics card will be able to mine at a far greater rate than even ten or twenty decently powered laptops.

It is important that as you build your mining rig that you spend money on the parts that are important, and minimize the costs on superfluous items. For example, you will not need computer monitors, keyboards and mice or speakers for these computers.

Ideally they do not have more than the parts necessary for efficient mining. You will of course need one monitor and a single keyboard and mouse to set up the mining on machines, but once the setup is complete the rest is handled automatically.

Motherboard

Assembling a modern computer might seem terrifying, but the truth is that it is quite similar to assembling Lego. Each part is a block that plugs into a central board called the 'motherboard'. This base component is where you will put your CPU/GPU and all of the other components that make up your computer. A motherboard is a necessary part, but not one that you should be spending all that much money on.

Even relatively inexpensive motherboards will serve fine for the purposes of mining. The most important aspect is that you buy a motherboard that is full size, as opposed to micro. The main consideration here is heat, and a smaller board does not fare as well as a larger one.

You can expect a motherboard to cost between $50 and $80, with preferable brands being ASUS, GIGABYTE and MSI. What's important is that your motherboard will be a determining factor in the type of central processing unit that you will use.

There are two main suppliers of processors, AMD and Intel. Depending on the motherboard, you will need the corresponding slot type and manufacturer. For example, an Intel LGA1155 board will only take Intel processors of that socket type. Do not let 'LGA1155' scare you – simply put, marketers have not realized the usefulness of catchy names for computer parts.

I strongly urge you to go with an Intel based motherboard capable of fitting an i3 or i5 processor. AMD processors are simply worse at handling heat, which is one of your main concerns for reducing the overhead cost of running a mining rig. You may first want to look at your choices of CPU and then base your motherboard decision off of what processor you will be purchasing.

As a general rule of thumb, processor costs are more fixed than motherboards. You may find an excellent sale on a motherboard, but it unlikely that the cost of a processor will change. Typically the manufacturer of CPUs will issue parts and never adjust the prices, only modifying pricing when new models of processors come out.

You should note that a motherboard will have many components already built into it. For example, your networking capability should be built into your motherboard. This is where you will also find your audio outputs and inputs for keyboard and mouse.

Power Supply

The power supply is the most important component of a mining rig. I have heard countless stories of people buying a cheap power supply only to see their mining rig burst into flames. This is not meant to be alarmist – power supplies are very safe, but they range in build quality greater than any other part on this list. The power supply is so essential because the computer will be running twenty-four hours a day, so stability is key.

I would recommend an EVGA, Thermaltake, or CORSAIR power supply. They come in different wattages, but for your needs, you must simply look for one that is 400 watts or greater. You should also note that power supplies are graded in terms of quality. Provided you buy a power supply that is silver or gold rated, you will be fine.

Additionally, the manufactures I have listed only make high quality power supplies, so even a bronze rated EVGA power supply will be sufficient. Expect the cost of a power supply to range between $50 and $80, depending on sales and promotions.

Power supplies should be changed out every eighteen months. All power supplies fail; the question is merely a matter of time, and how they will die. A poorly manufactured power supply will take all of the connected parts with it, meaning that an entire rig can be lost. A well-made power supply will simply stop working, meaning you can salvage all of the parts in the machine. You would simply need to replace the power supply to get it running again.

Since these machines are running at maximum load all of the time, an eighteen month period of use is to be expected. You can run them for longer, but you always risk a failure that may take out other parts with it.

Graphics Card (GPU)

The graphics card is the second most important part of your mining rig. This is where the true computational power comes into play. While a central processing unit can only handle a few calculations at a time, a graphics card can handle hundreds at the same time. It is a byproduct of their design, taking instructions from the CPU to power onscreen images. The relative power in each core of the GPU is low, but with so many of them they can mine much more efficiently than any CPU.

There are two main brands to buy from for graphics processors, NVidia and AMD. This is the same AMD that also makes CPUs, and for what it is worth the other main CPU manufacturer, Intel, owns NVidia. Both companies have good models of consumer video cards for mining. Most recently both companies have released new products that consume less power and are more efficient when it comes to heat.

There is a bit of a trade off in these two manufacturers. NVidia costs a bit more, and is not as fast as similar AMD cards, however they are more reliable overall, consume less power and produce drastically less heat. For my own rigs, I primarily use NVidia cards. This is merely because their cards were available to me before the latest line of AMD cards.

I would recommend that you either use a NVidia 1060 ($250) or an AMD 480 ($200). Both of these models have variations depending on the manufacturer of the card. For example you may see an EVGA 480, but this is the same base product as the one that AMD offers.

Without getting into too many details, the boards are free to be manufactured provided the companies get royalties for the technology. The primary difference is sometimes the clock speeds are increased, or the mounted cooling units are more efficient. There is no brand of either GPU that I would not recommend, and in fact I would just go with whatever is cheapest.

In these various models you will also see that they are differentiated based on the amount of memory that they have, coming in 3 and 6 GB versions for NVidia, and 4 and 8 GB versions for AMD. For the purposes of mining, the onboard video memory does not matter – buy the card with less memory as it will always be cheaper.

A GPU should be replaced once every two to three years, but the main catalyst for replacement should be that a new and more efficient model has been released. When a GPU dies, it simply stops working, so the build quality is not as essential as with a power supply.

It is my recommendation that if you start building mining rigs, you on occasion look at benchmarks for power efficiency in video cards. New cards come out roughly every year or so, with major revisions happening every two to four years – the latest major revisions were in 2016.

Central Processing Unit (CPU)

For processors you have a choice between Intel and AMD. What processor type you buy does not matter that much, as both are equally suitable for mining. What is important is that the socket type of the processor matches the motherboard that you buy. With this, it is my advice that you buy your motherboard and CPU at the same time, if only to ensure compatibility.

Like with video cards, the differences between the types of CPUs come down to heat and cost. AMD costs less but produces more heat. Intel costs more but produces less heat. Remember that more heat means more power consumption, and so you can trade the upfront cost for long term savings by going with Intel, or you can pay less now and go with AMD.

This is one of the more expensive parts of a mining rig, with the average cost of a processor being slightly over $200. The naming convention of the AMD processors is not as intuitive as the Intel system. I would suggest an i3 processor for Intel, which could cost as low as $150, or any AMD processor that is 'Bulldozer' or newer.

The upper limit for the cost of this part is $250, with the cheapest processor type coming in at $150. Other guides may suggest going with an i5 Intel processor, but the truth is that you don't really need this type of power. We are building a mining rig for home use, not a rig that will be joined with hundreds of other computers in a warehouse.

Memory (RAM)

The random access memory, or RAM, is a part that should not cost you more than $40 or $50. There are many different manufacturers of RAM, and I cannot recommend one brand over any other; that is because there is a consistent quality to RAM, which has more or less made it a commodity. You will need between 4 and 8 GB of system ram for efficient mining. 4 GB is fine in 2017, but by 2018 or 2019 you will likely want to have 8GB of RAM in your system.

This is an easily upgradeable part, so I would buy the cheapest and smallest amount as you get started. Please note that while the numbers and markings are the same, system RAM is very different from video card memory. One does not substitute the other, so even if you have a 3 GB video card, you will still need 4 GB of system RAM for your rig.

Storage

Storage is an essential part of any computer, but not one that you should spend a lot of money on. Storage options come in the form of hard drives (HDD) and solid state drives (SSD), with the latter being far more expensive. There has been a push for miners to move to SSD due to the lower power usage, but I have found the cost of SSDs to be so great that the upfront cost does not justify the long term power usage.

Any hard drive from any manufacturer will do – look for storage sizes of 80 GB up to 1 TB, and buy whatever part is cheapest. Note that hard drives do fail and that without a storage drive your rig will stop working. You will need to replace it if it fails, but you will not lose any of your cryptocurrency, as that is stored on the public ledger and not locally on your machine.

Operating System

Your options for operating systems are Windows or Linux, and I highly recommend the later. A Linux license is free and an image can be found online quite easily. To install an operating system like Linux, simply create a bootable flash drive by following the instructions provided by the specific version of Linux that you install. I would recommend Linux Red Hat or Ubuntu – you can think of these naming conventions as Windows 7, 10 etc.

They all have the same foundation but their interface is slightly different. Before you decide on the version of Linux that you want, I do suggest that you look at a compatibility chart to ensure your preferred cryptocurrency is listed. Once you have Linux installed, you must simply download the cryptocurrency client that you wish to mine. Install the client, set up an account and follow the instructions to start mining.

Chapter 18 How To Purchase Cryptocurrencies

Cryptocurrencies are digital assets that are gaining more international popularity as time progresses. These can be mined, bought, and traded over dedicated exchange platforms. There are also a number of different applications that can be used to conduct direct trades not to mention find cryptocurrency buyers and sellers all over the map.

For those who are interested in investing in these cryptocurrencies, one of the first things to think about is converting money into these digital currencies. The easiest way to do this is through a simple purchase transaction.

1.   Buy cryptocurrencies via exchange platforms.

Again, there are exchanges where these currencies can be traded in. Most of these exchange platforms also offer a variety of cryptocurrencies for sale. Keep in mind though that these currencies are in no way owned by the exchangers. Think of the latter as a commercial bank that stores, trades, and offers money to the public.

When you utilize an exchange, not only can you convert real money into cryptocurrencies but you can also convert them back when needed. It is also possible to use a particular cryptocurrency to purchase one of the other varieties. Considering the variety of services that you can avail of from an exchange, finding the one suitable to your needs is truly essential.

When choosing an exchange, the decision does not only boil down the transaction fees they charge or how many payment channels they can accommodate. There are certain exchanges that only accommodate a particular category of cryptocurrencies so you really want to have a clear decision as to what particular cryptocurrency you wish to invest in early on.

The most commonly traded cryptocurrency today is Bitcoin so if you are new to these digital currencies, it would be a safe bet to start with them. If you find your interest in those which have only been released recently, you might find it quite challenging to locate an exchange that has already updated its system to accommodate these. Not to say that there are no exchanges available. It is just that you have to be ready to spend more time during your search for exchanges.

Apart from this, do know that Bitcoins can be traded for a number of real-world currencies while other types of digital currencies may only be traded with Bitcoins. So it is also necessary that you be mindful of the different trading pairs that are being offered by your shortlisted exchanges.

Although it was mentioned earlier that service fees need not be the basis of your decision when it comes to selecting an exchange, it is still relevant in this entire process. Most of the time, beginners only consider the trade or transaction fees; these pertains to the percentage that the exchange earns per transaction. This fee can vary from one exchange to another. You will find some that charge small fees while others may be entitled to as much as 5% of your total earnings.

Aside from the trade fees, there are also standard usage fees (fixed monthly service fees) as well as deposit and withdrawal charges that you need to pay close attention to. Most of the time, the highest miscellaneous charge will come from withdrawals as the exchange transfers real money into your chosen channel. This is why it is important to find an exchange that has close ties with local financial institutions in your area as this ensures lower transfer fees.

Exchanges are not heavily regulated and this is a fact that you should never forget. There are those which have been able to stand the tests of time and continue to provide valuable services to cryptocurrency investors while there are some which have closed down for good. In the case of the latter, there have been reports of unfulfilled payments and this is why you need to do extensive research.

Aside from the exchanges' reputation, you also have to take a look at their security protocols. All of this information should be readily available online or in their websites. If you cannot find enough information about a particular exchange, that is your signal to start looking for a completely different platform.

2.   Buy cryptocurrencies via a cryptocurrency wallet.

A part of the cryptocurrency investment process involves the usage of a cryptocurrency wallet. There are exchanges that offer this added feature while others will require you to visit a third-party provider for your storage needs.

You will find that there are a number of these storage facilities that also offer direct buying and selling of cryptocurrencies. Unlike exchanges where the rates vary from seller to seller, with cryptocurrency wallets there usually is a fixed rate that applies for both purchasing and dispensing. All you have to do to make a purchase is to link your credit card or bank account information to your cryptocurrency wallet.

Upon first glance, it seems as if this option of purchasing cryptocurrencies is the best one to consider. But before you make any final decision on the matter, know that just like other methods available, purchasing coins through your digital wallet also has its fair share of pros and cons.

Let's start with why it is good to consider:

• Transactions are quick to accomplish here. You can compare it to any online shopping site where you choose a product, add it to your card, enter your payment details, and that is about it.

• Identity verification is a breeze as you simply have to link your payment information to the system to start making purchases.

• You can find ATMs that now cater to cryptocurrencies so you can directly buy coins there. Kiosks are also being developed for the same purpose and there is also an ongoing initiative to start offering cryptocurrencies in retail establishments like convenience stores and agencies such as post offices.

But it also has several points of concern:

• Transactions may be fast but there are limitations as to the trading pairs being offered by cryptocurrency wallets. This means that there may be real-world currencies that they will not accept.

• Your privacy may be at risk when you connect your personal information and payment details in the system. Cryptocurrencies are founded on the concept of trader anonymity but this is defeated by having transactions tied to your identity.

3. Buy cryptocurrencies via P2P

Cryptocurrencies can also be bought via peer-to-peer transactions. If you have a friend who owns coins that you want then you can ask them to sell and vice versa. The important thing here is finding a seller who is willing to part with their coins. There are exchanges that work simply by connecting buyers and sellers around the world so this is a good option to consider. There are also communities and forums that you can participate in if you wish to find these people by yourself.

Aside from your personal network and those from exchanges, you can also work with your wallet provider as some have local trading tools built into the system. Here, you will be connected to sellers within your area and you will be able to converse with them directly. If you make a purchase or vice versa, the transaction will immediately be reflected into your wallet.

You might be thinking how safe such transactions can be. Well, you can always use online tools, investor testimonials, and such to check the legitimacy of the seller. If you will be working on a platform for this, you will benefit from the ratings that each account holder has. But the decision will always be yours to make and the consequences yours to bear. So be careful and smart so that you find a trustworthy individual to work with.

Here are a couple more things that you should bear in mind when buying cryptocurrencies via P2P. If transactions are not to be done digitally, make sure that you transact in a public place. Meeting someone for the first time, for such a transaction can be scary and having tons of other people around will help safeguard you from the cons.

Online, be careful as there are phishing sites everywhere. Always go the extra mile and verify not only the individual's identity but the platform that you will be using for the transaction. This will ensure that your personal and financial information will be safe from prying eyes. Also be careful when it comes to phishing emails and such.

4.   Buy cryptocurrencies via credit card.

These days, thanks to the evolution of online payment channels and systems, you can also buy your chosen cryptocurrencies using your credit card. But do remember that just like with other things that you can purchase online, there still remain several risks when you charge purchases to your credit card.

The great thing about credit cards is that most of them, especially Visa and MasterCard, are accepted by all platforms and payments can be accommodated regardless of what home currency it is that you are using. This is because any monetary conversion can be accommodated by your home bank.

5.   Buy cryptocurrencies via wire.

You will find some individuals or exchanges for that matter that accept wire transfers as modes of payment. The problem though is that these transfers can take days to complete.

6.   Buy cryptocurrencies via online payment channels.

Online payment channels like PayPal, for example, can also be used to purchase cryptocurrencies. You have the option of linking your credit card to the system or using your internal wallet for the transaction. Do expect additional service fees here but do know that these fees actually protect you as these systems almost always come with dispute protocols wherein failed transactions or complaints will merit an investigation and may lead to your money being returned to your account.

7.   Buy cryptocurrencies via cash.

Especially for P2P arrangements, you can also use cash to purchase your chosen coins. In this case, you can choose to pay cash outright during a meet-up or use cash funds in a digital wallet during your transaction. Either way it is the quickest mode of payment available today, online or offline.

So there you have it. There are plenty of different ways by which you can purchase cryptocurrencies to start your investment journey with. Just make sure that you do your research before choosing a particular option. It will also be wise to try several methods out then determine which one works best in your favor.

Chapter 19 The Legitimacy of Cryptocurrency

When you think about it, just the name cryptocurrency suggests something cryptic or mysterious. Though growing in popularity, it still remains a mystery to a lot of people.

The core thought and main purpose of cryptocurrency was to have a quicker and cheaper method or moving funds on a global scale, without having to deal with banks or the government. Because of this, it has gained a lot of momentum from users who valued privacy and anonymity, though some of those users had less than noble reasons of their own.

But really, how legitimate is cryptocurrency and how safe is it to use?

Cryptocurrency has already been around for a few years, but it is still considered to be in the earlier stages of its development. There are many opinions regarding the legitimacy of cryptocurrency though most of them are baseless.

It would be quite difficult to actually answer the question of the legitimacy of cryptocurrency. Since a lot of users are able to successfully use and transact with cryptocurrency, you'd think that would be enough to consider it as legit. However, as it is decentralized by nature and it cannot be controlled by the government, then maybe it cannot be considered as legit.

Probably the best thing you can do is learn how to spot scams around cryptocurrency and how to protect yourself from them and take precautionary security measures.

How to Spot Cryptocurrency Scams

To be able to identify cryptocurrency scams, you'd have to be vigilant and aware of the warning signs. A lot of scams carry the same warning signs, making it a bit easier for you to spot them.

In looking for the perfect cryptocurrency to use, you would have to be aware of these points so that you won't fall into the hands of scammers who are just interested in getting your money.

- You are Given an Opportunity to "Get Rich Quick!"

Think about it, why would a total stranger help you get rich quick out of the blue? If you are presented with a chance to make a lot of money in a short amount of time, this is probably a scam. As what has been mentioned over and over again, cryptocurrency is in no way a get-rich-quick scheme so if you encounter something like this, just ignore it and move on.

- The Offer Seems Too Good to be True

When it comes to investing in cryptocurrency, if the offer seems too good to be true, it probably is. Offers which present returns which are double or triple the amount of your money are most likely just scams. Dealing with cryptocurrency takes a lot of time, effort and smart decision making, not just fast deals which are filled with empty promises.

- You Cannot Confirm What is Being Claimed

When you are given an offer or when you see an interesting kind of cryptocurrency wherein someone is communicating with you about all the benefits of signing up, do more research and see if you can confirm or verify what is being claimed. "Hidden" or "stealth" offers make no sense and are most likely scams.

- The Most Basic Data is Missing

In your search for the cryptocurrency which you will use, be mindful of all the information about the company or organization you plan to sign up with. Research the roots and history of the corporation which owns the cryptocurrency especially if it's new or it isn't that popular. If you notice that basic data- such as the owners of the company or the physical address of the office, are missing, it would be better to move on to more concrete options.

- Base of Operations in Another Country

If they claim that the main office or base of operations of the company is in a different country, be wary. It might happen to be in a country with very little regard for the law or a country which, conveniently, speaks a different language, one which you don't understand - making it difficult for you to establish good communication with them if any issues arise.

- Too Much False and "Good" Advertising

If the company which owns the cryptocurrency gives out too much information on how gallant and righteous they are, how they are only working towards selfless deeds and how enormous profits come as merely a bonus, it would be wise not to just jump on the wagon and invest everything you have. Again, do more research as things like this are most likely just a scam.

- You are Offered Higher Returns if you Invest More Initially

Often a mistake made by beginners, they are dazzled with offers of bigger profits, the more money they put in as they sign up. This is just not true. Scammers are able to entice newbies with offers like this before disappearing once the big amount of money has already been given to them.

- You are Given a Compensation Plan

This only works for salespeople who have to meet quotas in order to get higher commissions. This kind of strategy doesn't apply to investors so you won't be needing a compensation plan when you buy, use, trade or sell cryptocurrency as you'd just be using it for transactions to either send or receive money.

- You'd Have to Recruit More Investors to Earn

This is not how cryptocurrency works. In fact, one of the features is you will be able to enjoy your anonymity so if you are asked to recruit others, this is nothing but a scam.

- There is No Concrete Product

Of course you'd have to be able to see your money as cryptocurrency. Without it, you have nothing to show for your investment.

- All the Information About the Cryptocurrency is Unclear

By now you have a lot more information about cryptocurrency. If in your search to find the one you will invest in you encounter one which gives vague or unclear information, there's a very high likelihood that it's not real.

- You Cannot Exchange Your Cryptocurrency

You have to be able to exchange your cryptocurrency for fiat currency otherwise it would have no value. So make sure that you have this option before making an investment.

Since cryptocurrency is digital, it makes it easy for people with the right skills to simulate a kind of cryptocurrency along with a website where you can sign up for it. If you're not careful, you may be tricked into signing up on a site for a cryptocurrency that doesn't actually exist!

To avoid this, remember to be wary of signing up. Do your research and make sure the cryptocurrency exists and you will be able to use it.

Chapter 20 Safety Tips in Using Cryptocurrency

Being able to spot scams is pertinent when dealing with cryptocurrency so you don't end up losing money at the very beginning, before you even start using it. To improve on that, you could also benefit from safety tips in using cryptocurrency.

When you use these tips along with being aware of the scams and scammers which can entrap you, you may have an easier time joining the cryptocurrency market. Once in, you'd have to maintain your safety also by using some of the tips in this list.

These safety tips are designed to help you efficiently make use of your cryptocurrency so you can get the most out of it.

1. Use Different Wallets for Your Cryptocurrency

Since transactions are fast and easy, you can create multiple wallets for different purposes. Make separate wallets for cryptocurrency which you plan to send, cryptocurrency which you plan to save or cryptocurrency which you receive.

Since there is no limit to the number or wallets a person can own, take advantage of that and divide your cryptocurrency. If you do this, there would be a lesser chance of your cryptocurrency being compromised.

2. Never Use Web Wallets for Your Savings

Web wallets are prone to hacking and there have been recent cases wherein they have been compromised and robbed of all their contents.

Yes, they are convenient, but keeping your savings in them might not be the smartest choice. You can make use of web wallets for sending and receiving payments to enjoy their convenience while still trying to be safe.

3. Secure Your Identity

Never, EVER share your private keys to anyone. It would be like giving away the PIN to your ATM card. If you share this information to anyone, you are placing your identity and your privacy in danger. It would make gaining access to your account a lot easier for the wrong sort of people.

4. Go Offline

Keeping your cryptocurrency in a wallet which is stored in your computer would make you quite prone to attacks from hackers or viruses. To augment your security, you can keep your private key in an offline location like in a flash drive or written on a piece of paper. To gain access to your wallet, you'd have to manually enter your private key, which would take longer but if it would keep your cryptocurrency safe, why not?

5. Realize the Relevance of Backing Up

To be able to save all the information related to your cryptocurrency, you can back everything up on an external hard drive or flash drive. You can also encrypt your data if you know how to keep it private even if someone obtains your backup files somehow.

Taking these precautionary measures may be able to help you secure your cryptocurrency account, allowing you to freely conduct transactions and get the most out of your currency.

Chapter 21 Investing In Cryptocurrencies

Anyone, who's been following cryptocurrencies, will probably have witnessed the exponential rise in value of Bitcoin. He may become interested in investing in digital currencies. It's understandable. However, for anyone, who wants to invest in cryptocurrencies, he must first study their ins and outs.

If a person wants to earn money from these digital currencies, he must see it not as investing but as speculating. A cryptocurrency can be a powerful way of conducting business in the future. However, no one can really tell if it can sustain its value right now because it's still in its early stages although there is a growing number of merchants and users who adopt it but the demand is still not large enough to consider it a legitimate trade. As such, trading cryptocurrencies isn't really an investment but a speculation.

Currently, the value of any currency is vulnerable to speculation by new speculators as well as those individuals who have been in possession of a cryptocurrency for a while. The ups and downs of the market are precisely caused by these speculators because speculating is actually a zero-sum game wherein somebody is left holding the bag at the end of the day. Therefore, a person must exercise caution in putting his money in any cryptocurrency. He mustn't invest his life savings in it.

It is possible to lose the cryptocurrency through theft. Some hacker or scammer may take hold of digital wallet if the owner isn't careful. It is imperative that secure wallet software is used. WarpWallet and Coinbase are known providers of a secure digital wallet. Furthermore, exchanges shouldn't be trusted especially if no reputable entity is backing any of them. Strong passwords must be used. As much as possible, the 2-factor authentication must be used. Sketchy screensavers mustn't be downloaded. It is better to be paranoid when protecting the digital coins.

A bad trader us characterized by his inability to stomach sudden market drops. He usually buys when the market is on an uptrend then sells if it's on a downtrend. It is actually better to think of the money as "probably gone". This way, the person can easily deal with any sharp price drops when trading cryptocurrencies. Any sudden price drop must be taken advantage of. Because the cryptocurrency market is still small, it is best to keep track of different digital currencies to take advantage of arbitrage.

It is also important to take advantage of market swings in a stabilizing and positive way. An individual must be sober and careful if he wants to earn money from cryptocurrencies. The market actually follows a pattern. If the digital currency is featured in the news, the price will be increase because day traders get into the cryptocurrency. These people make money then start selling their inventory. Once the value of the cryptocurrency falls, they sell what they have so the price falls. Once the price goes down, some people will get into it and the cycle continues. However, there is no guarantee that this pattern will go on.

The value of any digital currency can sustain itself if there are more adopters who will continuously use it. However, it may take time before the real effects can overcome the results of speculation. Speculation can be an opportunity for any person who wants to eventually make money from cryptocurrencies. However, it shouldn't be regarded as a day job. It isn't even a get-rich-quick scheme. If anybody wants to try cryptocurrencies, he must be responsible and careful.

Chapter 22 Advantages Of Cryptocurrency

1.   Built-in Scarcity May Support Value

Most cryptocurrencies are hardwired for scarcity – the source code specifies how many units can ever exist. In this way, cryptocurrencies are more like precious metals than fiat currencies. Like precious metals, they may offer inflation protection unavailable to fiat currency users.

2.   Loosening of Government Currency Monopolies

Cryptocurrencies offer a reliable means of exchange outside the direct control of national banks, such as the U.S. Federal Reserve and European Central Bank. This is particularly attractive to people who worry that quantitative easing (central banks' "printing money" by purchasing government bonds) and other forms of loose monetary policy, such as near-zero inter-bank lending rates, will lead to long-term economic instability.

In the long run, many economists and political scientists expect world governments to co-opt cryptocurrency, or at least to incorporate aspects of cryptocurrency (such as built-in scarcity and authentication protocols) into fiat currencies. This could potentially satisfy some cryptocurrency proponents' worries about the inflationary nature of fiat currencies and the inherent insecurity of physical cash.

3.   Self-Interested, Self-Policing Communities

Mining is a built-in quality control and policing mechanism for cryptocurrencies. Because they're paid for their efforts, miners have a financial stake in keeping accurate, up-to-date transaction records – thereby securing the integrity of the system and the value of the currency.

4.   Robust Privacy Protections

Privacy and anonymity were chief concerns for early cryptocurrency proponents, and remain so today. Many cryptocurrency users employ pseudonyms unconnected to any information, accounts, or stored data that could identify them. Though it's possible for sophisticated community members to deduce users' identities, newer cryptocurrencies (post-Bitcoin) have additional protections that make it much more difficult.

5.   Harder for Governments to Exact Financial Retribution

When citizens in repressive countries run afoul of their governments, said governments can easily freeze or seize their domestic bank accounts, or reverse transactions made in local currency. That's not possible with cryptocurrencies, whose decentralized nature – funds and transaction records are stored in numerous locations around the world – effectively prevents state seizure. It's a bit of an oversimplification, but using cryptocurrency is like having access to a theoretically unlimited number of offshore bank accounts.

6.   Generally Cheaper Than Traditional Electronic Transactions

The concepts of block keys, private keys, and wallets effectively solve the double-spending problem, ensuring that new cryptocurrencies aren't abused by tech-savvy crooks capable of duplicating digital funds. Cryptocurrencies' security features also eliminate the need for a third-party payment processor – such as Visa or PayPal – to authenticate and verify every electronic financial transaction.

In turn, this eliminates the need for mandatory transaction fees to support those payment processors' work – since miners, the cryptocurrency equivalent of payment processors, earn new currency units for their work in addition to optional transaction fees. Cryptocurrency transaction fees are generally less than 1% of the transaction value, versus 1.5% to 3% for credit card payment processors and PayPal.

7.   Fewer Barriers and Costs to International Transactions

Cryptocurrencies don't treat international transactions any differently than domestic transactions. Transactions are either free or come with a nominal transaction fee, no matter where the sender and recipient are located. This is a huge advantage relative to international transactions involving fiat currency, which almost always have some special fees that don't apply to domestic transactions – such as international credit card or ATM fees. And direct international money transfers can be very expensive, with fees sometimes exceeding 10% or 15% of the transferred amount.

Chapter 23 Cons Of Cryptocurrency

1.   Lack of Regulation Facilitates Black Market Activity

Probably the biggest drawback and regulatory concern around cryptocurrency is its ability to facilitate illicit activity. Many gray and black market online transactions are denominated in Bitcoin and other cryptocurrencies. For instance, the infamous "dark web" marketplace Silk Road used Bitcoin to facilitate illegal drug purchases and other illicit activities before being shut down in 2014. Cryptocurrencies are also increasingly popular tools for money laundering – funneling illicitly obtained money through a "clean" intermediary to conceal its source.

The same strengths that make cryptocurrencies difficult for governments to seize and track allow criminals to operate with relative ease – though, it should be noted, the founder of Silk Road is now behind bars, thanks to a years-long DEA investigation.

2.   Potential for Tax Evasion in Some Jurisdictions

Since cryptocurrencies aren't regulated by national governments and usually exist outside their direct control, they naturally attract tax evaders. Many small employers pay employees in bitcoin and other cryptocurrencies to avoid liability for payroll taxes and help their workers avoid income tax liability, while online sellers often accept cryptocurrencies to avoid sales and income tax liability.

According to the IRS, the U.S. government applies the same taxation guidelines to all cryptocurrency payments by and to U.S. persons and businesses. However, many countries don't have such policies in place. And the inherent anonymity of cryptocurrency makes some tax law violations, particularly those involving pseudonymous online sellers (as opposed to an employer who puts an employee's real name on a W-2 indicating their bitcoin earnings for the tax year), difficult to track.

3.   Potential for Financial Loss Due to Data Loss

Early cryptocurrency proponents believed that, if properly secured, digital alternative currencies promised to support a decisive shift away from physical cash, which they viewed as imperfect and inherently risky. Assuming a virtually uncrackable source code, impenetrable authentication protocols (keys) and ade□uate hacking defenses (which Mt. Gox lacked), it's safer to store money in the cloud or even a physical data storage device than in a back pocket or purse.

However, this assumes that cryptocurrency users take proper precautions to avoid data loss. For instance, users who store their private keys on single physical storage devices suffer irreversible financial harm when the device is lost or stolen. Even users who store their data with a single cloud service can face loss if the server is physically damaged or disconnected from the global Internet (a possibility for servers located in countries with tight Internet controls, such as China).

4.   Potential for High Price Volatility and Manipulation

Many cryptocurrencies have relatively few outstanding units concentrated in a handful of individuals' (often the currencies' creators and close associates) hands. These holders effectively control these currencies' supplies, making them susceptible to wild value swings and outright manipulation – similar to thinly traded penny stocks.

5.   Often Can't Be Exchanged for Fiat Currency

Generally, only the most popular cryptocurrencies – those with the highest market capitalization, in dollar terms – have dedicated online exchanges that permit direct exchange for fiat currency. The rest don't have dedicated online exchanges, and thus can't be directly exchanged for fiat currencies. Instead, users have to convert them into more commonly used cryptocurrencies, such as Bitcoin, before fiat currency conversion. This suppresses demand for, and thus the value of, some lesser-used cryptocurrencies.

6.   Limited to No Facility for Chargebacks or Refunds

Although cryptocurrency miners serve as quasi-intermediaries for cryptocurrency transactions, they're not responsible for arbitrating disputes between transacting parties. In fact, the concept of such an arbitrator violates the decentralizing impulse at the heart of modern cryptocurrency philosophy. This means that you have no one to appeal to if you're cheated in a cryptocurrency transaction – for instance, paying upfront for an item you never receive. Though some newer cryptocurrencies attempt to address the chargeback/refund issue, solutions remain incomplete and largely unproven.

By contrast, traditional payment processors such as Visa, MasterCard, and PayPal often step in to resolve buyer-seller disputes. Their refund, or chargeback, policies are specifically designed to prevent seller fraud.

Chapter 24 Understanding The Risks

Having a basic understanding of cryptocurrencies, you may be wondering why they haven't reached mainstream society yet or why we aren't being pushed further to use them. They are not without their risks and while there is an extensive list, we will be covering the three most significant.

Some Technologies Will Fail

Keep in mind that cryptocurrencies, while also a replacement for regular currency, also have a software component to them. This means they are created by human hands either individually or as a company and just like many companies that were found insolvent during the dot-com bust such as Webyan or Pets.com, these technologies are not immune to failure.

Some cryptocurrencies have seen tremendous growth, some in just a few short months with increases of several thousand percent. Unfortunately, this is largely due to speculation and ignorant investors attempting to cash in on the hype. Similar to how many people over invested in internet companies in the late nineties and early 2000s with the assumption that the internet would change the world of business. Of course, we know that it most certainly did but keep in mind that many of those companies were terrible investments and the ignorance combined with hype caused these companies to have over inflated values before going under.

Taking this experience and applying it to the world of cryptocurrency, you will need understand that while there are some great investments out there that will change the world, others will likely implode dramatically, taking your savings with you, similar to software stock in the early 2000s. You will also need to be aware of the large number of scam coins out there that can be seen as the equivalent of penny stocks with no real business model and are hollow. Anyone with a bit of programming experience can create a new cryptocurrency meaning you will need to be able to separate the scams from undervalued currencies that could later be realised. Have a risk management strategy in place and know your odds.

It Requires Technical Savvy

Not everyone can jump right in and understand cryptocurrencies. Many of these currencies were developed by experienced programmers and similar to the case of Linux, you will still need a bit of technical knowledge to know how to use it. While you don't exactly need to know how to code, you will at the very least need to be a little computer savvy in order to engage in cryptocurrency trading. For those who are not too good with computers, it may be best to wait until there are more user-friendly interfaces before getting started to avoid making any serious mistakes.

This is not to say that inexperienced people should not get involved in cryptocurrency trading. Though if you don't have certain skills on the computer, you could risk losing a great deal of money in a short amount of time. If you feel that you are out of your depth in trading, it might be best to find someone you trust to help you with your trades and ensure that they themselves know what to look for.

There's a Lot of Broker and Technology Risk

As with any new and emerging technology, there can be a lot uncertainty surrounding how the technology will be traded at scale as well as how brokers and the software will operate given unpredicted events. If you can imagine the risk behind the brokers that are trading in forex being somewhat risky, you will need to think of cryptocurrency brokers as being double that risk. This isn't to say that they are shady or unscrupulous, it is just that with a technology so new, there is a lot we don't know and certain events can be very unpredictable. When you think of the grand scheme of trading, cryptocurrency falls somewhere in the middle, there are many more risky investment vehicles and while cryptocurrency is not the safest available, the reliability of it will improve as the technology develops.

A good piece of advice towards minimizing your risk is to avoid having too much coin under the watch of your broken and instead move the coinage to your personal wallet as soon as possible.

Chapter 25 Trading Strategies

With a now clear idea of what cryptocurrency trading entails and the basics behind assessing what makes a particular cryptocurrency a hidden gem, you are now ready to start making some money through trading digital currency. In order to do this, you will need a rundown of some of the more specific strategies and technical available to you. While this section will provide you with some ideas in order to start making money as an altcoin trader, it is in no way a comprehensive guide and there are many more strategies worth exploring once you have perfected these few. See what works for you and what you feel comfortable with.

Getting in on the Ground Floor

Almost all coins will start off with a very low entry price and as they become more successful, they will rise in value. While this may not be true for all coins, especially those undertaking an ICO whereby they start with a quite a valuation, you can see some incredible profits by seeing the benefits and potential of a new coin early on in its life. In order to do this, you will need to get in long before the coin has heated up with demand and once the coin does start to rise in success, you will be able to reap the rewards as the value dramatically rises.

This strategy does have its disadvantages though since many of the early coins carry the most risk. There will be uncertainty surrounding the technology used by the coin and there is a chance the technology may not have even finished development. This can mean there is very little evidence to analyse whether the coin will ultimately be successful or not so you could essentially be gambling based on the speculation that the coin will rise in value. Keep in mind though that cryptocurrency trading in itself is a high risky endeavour with very lucrative rewards. It is best to spread your investment capital over a large number of diversified ventures if you do choose to go down this route, minimising your risk in the event that some of your investments may fall through.

Another way you can capitalize on this approach is to take part in mining. When some coins are launched, they have a period where they are available to mine before being added to adding trading exchanges. This allows you to get involved at the very early stage well before many other traders take their piece of the pie. You can keep track of the latest launches by following announcement boards which are located on sites such as Bitcointalk and Cryptocointalk as well as a dedicated website such as Altcoin Calender.

Buy the Rumour, Sell the News

With altcoins being highly volatile, any news in the market can have an enormous affect with big swings from anything such as new announcements, feature releases as well as partnerships. Things like announcements can cause a price to drive up immediately but there is something many traders don't realise is that these announcements have already been adjusted for the price to fluctuate as a result of the news. For this reason, buying in after the news has been announced can be a case of following the crowd and can result in you purchasing an overpriced asset and while it can still be profitable, it is best to consider the information on a case by case basis rather than just following the news. Instead you should be doing what you can do predict the news and what happens next and once the decisions are made and the news is brought out to the general public, you will profit more than if you were a late coming to the market w after the price has already spiked.

Activist Investing

Drawing comparison towards other traditional markets such as stocks and forex, you will find that cryptocurrency markets are unique in the opportunity that they offer individual investors as they are able to become involved in assisting their investments towards becoming more successful. Some traders, once they have purchased a large volume of a particular coin, will become an active member of the community of users, offering their support and helping to promote the coin to other investors as well as brainstorming and critiquing new ideas in the community forums, networking to create new opposites even getting involved in developing new code through open source programs.

Getting involved with your investment is a great way to put some of skills to use and help improve the success of the particular coin, especially if you genuinely enjoy doing so. Being involved at this level will also expose you to information that you can use in order to make more informed decisions about where the coin is heading and its viability in the future.

When you are involved at this level it is important to remain objective in your decisions and not let your passion for a project cloud your vision, especially if the market conditions are stating otherwise. When you have an indication to sell at the right time, it is best to make that decision to sell your holdings rather than hold onto them only to regret it later. You will want to ensure that you leave your emotions at the door when trading to avoid affecting your decisions and making costly mistakes.

Don't Fight the Market

When involved in smaller markets, there is a strong likelihood that the decisions you make and the orders you carry out may have an effect on the movement of those markets. This could even be through small offers that drive the price higher as others attempt to beat your price by making their own offers. Keep in mind that you will want to avoid using this to your advantage as it can be quite costly unless you know what you are doing.

An example of this is when a trader might see the value of a coin they are holding going down. What they will then try and do is place extra buy orders, not because they believe that the coin is a worthwhile investment but because they want to support the price and avoid having it go down further. This doubling down attempt is very risky and can lead to you purchasing more than what you had intended of a declining asset. Always keep in mind where the market is heading and move with the market, not against it.

Contrarianism

A contrarian trader will always count on the fact that markets will be subject to fluctuations as traders overreact and the market will always follow through with a correction. The logic here is that because everyone else is selling, the price offered is likely to be due to this overselling and that the right time to buy is now. Similarly, if everyone else is buying then the best time sell would be while the demand is hot as the correction would not be far off once the market calm down. Contrarianism is a long-term strategy and in order to do it successfully, you will find that there will a period of significant losses before the prices correct themselves and you will be able to make a profit. This can be a highly dangerous strategy when dealing with highly volatile as cryptocurrency and is not recommended for beginners however if you have some funds that are not averse to some risk, it can be quite lucrative when successful.

Trend Trading

As a medium-term strategy, identifying and following trans can be done virtually at any time scam meaning it can be quite a flexible strategy. You will need to ensure before you take advantage of a trend, that the trend you are analysing is congruent with the timescale you have decided on. There is a principle that needs to be taken into account to ensure that you follow the trends correctly and that is if there is a general upwards trend in a price, it is most likely going to continue following that trend in the foreseeable future than to start trending in the opposite direction. You are able to utilize your technical analysis skills at this point when treading trends as this can assist you identifying potential turning points and prevent you from purchasing at the peak of a trend or selling at the bottom of a downtrend.

Swing Trading

As a short-term strategy, swing trading is one which attempts to take advantage of the peaks and troughs of price rather than following a smooth path. The concept of this is to be able to pinpoint exactly where the bottom of the short-term price wings is in order to buy at the lowest end out of the cycle only to resell at the high end of the peak once the price spikes back upwards, repeating the process multiple times. As cryptocurrency markets fluctuate rapidly and highly volatile, there can be a significant spread between the buy and sell prices in contrast to some of the traditional markets. As a swing trader, you are able to act as a 'market maker' in order to make additional profit from this spread. For example, if the spread is quite a large percentage in comparison to the fees charged by the exchange, then this should be taken into consideration. It is recommended though that you are always aware that in the lower volume markets, there can be some delay in exiting your positions and this can cause some difference in the spread that you may not have predicted.

Being a Whale

With those cryptocurrency markets that have a low market capitalisation of around $10 - 20,000, even a smaller trader with just a few thousand dollars can see themselves as a whale, making big changes to the market even though their capital is low compared to some of the other markets.

The advantages of this can be seen when buying into a very low value coin that may have some potential that has not been revealed to the mainstream market. The big fish in the small pond analogy can be hugely profitable for the dedicated trader but beware as this can also backfire dangerously. You may find that your purchases alone can have an effect on the price of the coin. This can be profitable in that these coins could now have a greater value than you had originally paid for them despite the fact you only just carried out the purchase, however you will need to keep in mind there may not be too many buyers in this market either meaning you could be holding the bag for a significant period of time and perhaps even permanently in the case that the coin could be abandoned or found worthless.

When carrying out this strategy it is important to take a look at the volume. Even if a coin has a very low valuation yet still has a high level of volume, then this can be an indication that you can get involved and drive up the price but even then, it is still highly recommended that you do your research into the technology to ensure that the coin you are purchasing has potential. Be aware also that it is possible for people to fake volume on an exchange by manipulating the market themselves so research in this instance is key.

Being Careful

While altcoin trading can be incredible exciting, fun, interesting and very lucrative financially, it is still carries plenty of inherent risk. While this has been mentioned numerous times throughout this book, it is worth mentioning in order to protect many newcomers to the market who are unsure about whether they should get started. Never risk more than you can afford to lose and rather than getting involved in trading purely for the money, get involved simply to have some fun and to develop your skills. There is a high chance you will lose money when you are just starting out and even the most experienced of traders find themselves having bad days. As you continue to trade, you will learn more about what to do look for and as you develop your strategies, you will start to not only regain what you have lost but also make a handsome profit as well.

Chapter 26 The Future of Cryptocurrencies

The cryptocurrency market is currently in a state of extreme fluctuation with more than 100 different types all trying to make their mark on the market despite the fact that only a handful are seeing even a small amount of adoption, which means the future of cryptocurrencies is extremely hard to determine. With that being said, there are some things that can be intuited based on how things are currently going.

Enhanced scrutiny

When it first arrived on the scene, one of bitcoin's main benefits were its high degree of decentralization and the fact that transactions could be completed with almost complete anonymity. The internet took advantage of this fact and immediately began using it as a means of purchasing all sorts of illegal things off of the darknet, most publicly from the Silk Road marketplace. Now that it has become somewhat more mainstream, regulatory and other government agencies including the Department of Homeland Security, the Federal Bureau of Investigations, the Securities and Exchange Commission and the Financial Crimes Enforcement Network are all taking a closer look.

This increased level of scrutiny first started building in 2013 when the Financial Crimes Enforcement Network first issued a rule that stated virtual currency exchanges were defined as money service businesses which means they could be regulated by the government. This was soon followed by the Department of Homeland Security freezing the accounts of the largest Bitcoin exchange, known as Mt. Gox, that were held by Wells Fargo, under concerns that it broke money laundering laws.

More recently in April of 2017, the Securities and Exchange Commission denied an application to allow an official exchange traded fund for bitcoin, a move that cost the cryptocurrency a fair amount of its market price, though it quickly recovered and went on to reach an all-time high. The SEC has since said that it would review it rejection decision which was accepted and only time will tell what the end result will be.

This has left bitcoin, and by extension all cryptocurrencies, in a bit of a paradoxical position, the more popular that they become the greater degree of government scrutiny and regulation they face which flies in the face of the reason they were initially conceived to begin with. Furthermore, while the number of merchants, both online and off, who accept the currency is expanding, it still represents a slim fraction of what would be needed in order to ensure true mainstream acceptance. In order for this to occur, their relative complexity compared to more traditional currencies would need to be curtailed as well.

For a cryptocurrency to aspire to true mainstream status and become a part of the incumbent financial system it will need to satisfy a wide variety of criteria. It would still need to be mathematically complex enough to supply the security that is required while still being easy for the average person to wrap their heads around. It would need to be decentralized enough to meet its original purpose, but only in a way that didn't make it a natural choice for money laundering, tax evasion and various other unsavory activities. This means that the cryptocurrencies of the future might be more an amalgamation of its current form and the more traditional types of fiat currencies.

Expansion of smart contract technology

While the exact way that cryptocurrencies are going to be utilized in the future is up in the air, their underlying technology is equally poised to make a big dent on the future. Currently blockchains are primarily used to transmit financial data but platforms like Ethereum are already looking to change that. This means they offer a wide variety of promises as to what the future can hold.

While non-financial blockchains are currently few and far between, the easiest way to see how they can be used in the future is to look at a basic financial example. Automated deductions from your checking account by your bank work along similar lines. The deduction comes out of your account without any action on your part and the bank can set up these deductions without your consent. This is precisely why the technology was created in the first place, to take control of these systems out of control of incumbent forces. In the future, there will likely be no way to submit changes to your account without your permission, largely because there will be no centralized force with a desire to do so.

Legal uses: When it comes to dealing with the legalese that fills most traditional contracts, it can be difficult for those without a law degree to make heads or tails out of who owes what to whom and how these clauses will come into effect. Smart contracts have the potential to cut through this legal red tape in a big way by automating parts of the process based on communal blockchains. They can ensure that x happens only if y happens first and is verified through the appropriate third party. There would be no need for this boilerplate type of content simply because it will all be handled automatically.

Besides just making the process more efficient, and simpler all around, smart contracts will also have the benefit of ensuring that everyone with access to a given contract can easily determine if a given event has taken place as well as when the event took place. There will be no room for disagreement as everything that occurs will be clearly outlined in block form and timestamped besides. Certain contracts will never take this step, however, specifically those that are required to uphold a great degree of secrecy.

Additionally, smart contracts can help real contracts stay up to date much more easily when it comes to various operating parameters. As such, if a timeframe or a monetary amount needs to be updated throughout a given negotiation, the changes can just be made to the underlying smart contract which will allow all relevant parties to act much more confidently in knowing that they can make changes without costly additional lawyer visits without sacrificing the binding nature of a traditional contract.

This, in turn, means that fewer intermediary players will be required to ensure that the paper version of the digital contract remain updated while still operating at speeds even the fastest courier couldn't hope to match. The binary nature of smart contracts also means they could also be used when it comes to extremely high-dollar contracts that typically require the use of a third party escrow service as all relevant parties will have a clear understanding of what requirements will need to be met in order for the money to be transferred with no room for personal bias.

Financial sector: When it comes to the financial sector then smart contracts are likely going to see use when it comes to managing the workflow and approval process inherent in settlement generation and trade clearing scenarios. Trades and transfers that happen as the result of a settlement can also be automated as well. Additionally, coupon payments that will be generated after bonds expire will also likely be automated through the use of smart contracts.

Smart contracts are also likely to be generated when it comes to paying out insurance claims and will be able to automatically do so once various binary factors are met. This will remove the need for insurance adjusters from the equation along with the need for personal opinion entirely as internet enabled cars will be able to report the facts and then smart contracts will pay out based on the specifics of a given policy. Insurance premiums could also then be set to run based on smart contracts as your insurance company could then monitor your vehicle to determine whether or not you are a safe driver.

Healthcare: Smart contracts have a potentially robust future ahead when it comes to tracking medical records and patients and can be used to automatically update the specifics related to individual patient care, removing the potential for human error from the process entirely which is typically magnified as a patient moves throughout the hospital. Preliminary research into this functionality by major hospital chains show that it could easily decrease clerical errors by upwards of 40 percent, especially during emergency scenarios.

Furthermore, as personal smart contracts become more common, your personal smart contract will be able to track your health information as you move throughout your day to day life, keeping tabs on your overall level of fitness and transferring these details to your primary care physician as needed. They will also help when it comes to making medical studies more efficient as those in the study can have their data automatically transferred to the research team while also making payments to the subjects at the same time. A personal medical smart contract could even be connected to a personal fitness tracker and it could then dole out rewards once you have hit certain milestones.

Redefine industry: Smart contracts will soon be able to monitor the energy that electric cars use and automatically deduct any power station use from your personal checking account. They will also soon be able to automatically provide updates for common clerical information based on a number of predefined indicators. It will even be able to release information to approved parties after it recognizes that specific digital signatures have been obtained.

Furthermore, it will be able to improve how supply chain details are documented and products will be free to move from one location to the next as quickly as possible while their locations are tracked and updated as they move along the route in question. They will even be able to authorize payment for the goods after they have reached their final destination. The same goes for port, promise and credit payments as they apply to bills of lading.

Consumers: As more and more manufacturers start utilizing blockchain technology the history of every given product will grow longer and more detailed as a result until even consumers will be able to easily tell the route each of the products they use took from the factory, to the store to their homes.

On the consumer side of things, perhaps the biggest change soon to come is the ease with which peer-to-peer transactions will be accomplished.

Once smart contract technology becomes common then users will be able to pay one another for goods and services, of course, but they will also be able to do a wide variety of other tasks such as exchange insurance information or to supply one another with energy credits. This, in turn, will lead to a shift in the lending market as smart contracts will be able to be used to automatically connect lenders and borrowers based on the factors that each party determines beforehand.

Voting: Finally, due to their clearly defined and extremely difficult to forge nature, smart contracts make a natural choice for improving the speed and ease of the voting process. Assuming that the smart contract in question was programed properly, it should be able to verify the status of individual voters, tally votes and even automatically notify the winners in local, state and even national elections, all without having to involve humans who might have a vested interest in seeing an election fall one way or another. Once all the kinks have been worked out, it will be impossible for incidents like the US presidential election of 2000 to happen ever again.

As you can see, while smart contract technology is only just now starting to see any type of usage thanks to the Ethereum platform, their sheer number of uses point to a future where they are used ubiquitously. The sheer range of uses means that the sooner you start defining what they are going to mean for you and how you can use them for the better, the more effective you will be in the new world they are creating. Look to the future and dream big.

Conclusion

Modern-day technology continues to improve day in and day out. And apart from the development of various devices, we too are in an age where digital currencies are created.

Cryptocurrencies are digital assets that hold value. They can be used to make purchases online and offline. They can also be held as investments. Functioning closely like traditional stocks, these are great financial tech instruments for those who want to earn a passive income on the side.

There are different elements though that you need to familiarize yourself with before investing in these cryptocurrencies. Doing your research and studying up on the different coin types, exchanges, wallets, and components will ensure that your transactions run safely.

After reading this book, I hope that you've gained ample knowledge about cryptocurrencies to be able to find enough confidence to get started. Just make sure that you do not act hastily as you are still participating in a monetary market.

In this case, it is important that you take your time, practice, and of course, have fun.

The next step is to find some coins to buy, an exchange to try, and a wallet to keep them well secured. Good luck!

Finally, if you enjoyed this book, please consider leaving a review. Reviews are one of the easiest ways to support the work of independent authors!